Sheet Metal Work

R.E.Wakeford

Special Interest Model Books

Special Interest Model Books Ltd.
P.O. Box 327
Poole
Dorset
BH15 2RG
England

First published by Argus Books 1985
Reprinted in 1987, 1989, 1994, 1996, 1999

This edition published by Special Interest Model Books Ltd, 2002
Reprinted 2005 and 2006, 2007, 2009, 2010, 2012, 2014

ISBN 978-0-85242-849-8

www.specialinterestmodelbooks.co.uk

Printed and bound in Malta by Melita Press

Contents

Introduction

Model engineers, D.I.Y. enthusiasts and other amateur home craftsmen are, from time to time, called upon to work with sheet metal. It is at such people that this book has been aimed. During its preparation I have tried to bear in mind that in this situation working conditions may be less than ideal with limited funds and equipment. Readers may well be people to whom metalworking is a fresh subject, so processes are described with the newcomer in mind but with the hope that more experienced workers may find in them something of value.

In spite of my comments above it is not uncommon to find quite well-equipped home workshops. Also many local authorities now run evening classes in model engineering and metalworking subjects. These give the amateur worker access to much more sophisticated equipment than he, or she, is likely to have at home. For these reasons, more advanced equipment and processes have not been ignored if they may be of use in the normal run of 'home-type' work.

Where dimensions have been quoted, the metric system has been used because this is becoming increasingly common. However, the Imperial system is preferred by many, and is likely to be with us for a long time yet, so equivalent measurements have been given in brackets after the metric ones whenever relevant.

Any opinions expressed are sincerely held in the light of my experience as a teacher of craft subjects* and as a home workshop and model railway enthusiast.

I hope that the information contained in this book will be of help and assistance to as many people as possible Home metalcraft is a fascinating and absorbing hobby.

R. E. Wakeford

*The author is a technology teacher at Ashcombe School, Dorking

CHAPTER 1

Tools

There are two generally accepted ways to start a book about a craft subject. One is to commence by considering the materials to be used, the other is to look at the tools required. I have adopted the latter approach with the idea that the possession of a few of the basic tools for the subject will permit practice and experiment with scrap material. From an amateur point of view, this would permit experience to be gained as to what is suitable and workable before spending hard-earned cash on lumps of metal.

The tools and equipment described here are mostly of the more basic nature for sheet metalworking. More specialised ones will be considered as the processes for which they are used are described.

Average model engineer and D.I.Y. enthusiasts will probably already possess some, or even much, of the equipment described. In these cases only a few items will need to be added to the workshop stock of tools. Some items like blocks and formers cannot, normally, be obtained commercially and need to be made to suit the work in hand.

The Bench

For any type of craft work a good bench on which to work is really essential. The main requirements here are that it should be heavy and robust. If making your own bench use substantial sizes of material and the strongest methods of jointing available to you.

General choice of material really comes down to wood or metal. Of the two wood is probably the best choice. Metal benches (usually made of steel) tend to be noisy and cold to work on in winter, but they are better if welding or brazing work is going to be carried out. I suppose the ideal is to have a bench made of each material, but many people will not have the time, money or room to adopt the ideal. Therefore, wood is probably the best choice with, perhaps, a steel sheet kept to cover it with when heating processes are being used. For some time I used this means to protect a wooden bench when arc welding. The steel sheet was the rear floor pan from an accident damaged estate car. Such things can often be obtained very cheaply from scrap dealers.

Quite good benches can be made or built upon old items of domestic furniture. Chests of drawers and kitchen tables can be used to make sound benches, but if this approach is used, try to choose something that is strongly made.

If making your own bench, ideally the frame and legs should be made from a hard wood like oak or beech with a surface of thick softwood planks. This is a fairly expensive option and I am sure most people will use softwood, such as pine, for the whole lot.

There is another satisfactory construction method that may be used and will permit thinner material to be used for legs and framework. That is to fix the bench to the wall of the workshop.

If using this method, make sure that the workshop walls are sufficiently strong. Many of us use garden sheds for workshops and my own use of a bench fixed to the walls of such a workshop showed that it is all too easy to set walls shaking when sawing and filing.

Whatever your choice of bench there are some important dimensions to bear in mind.

The working surface needs to be as large as space will permit, especially if one needs to lay a sheet of metal flat for marking out. Size of work to be under-taken will also have a bearing on this, but remember you can do small work on a large bench, but not the other way round!

A more critical dimension is height. Sheet metalworking does not involve so much general filing and sawing as other types of metalwork, but even so these processes are often required. Therefore I will repeat the rule over height that I have always accepted. This is that the bench surface should be of such a height that with an item held in the vice and being filed the top of the vice should be level with the worker's elbow (see Fig. 1).

To my mind, this is the most important consideration of all with regard to benches. It is the big argument in favour of making your own, since we are not all the same height. Also it is an argument against using old kitchen tables and the like, because these always seem to be too low. This will cause backache after a working session of any length.

It is a good idea, if the top surface of the bench is made from planks, to cover these with hardboard sheet. This gives a nice smooth surface on which to work, and if it is held down with steel or aluminium screwed around the edges, or lightly pinned, it can be removed and replaced when worn out. The bench

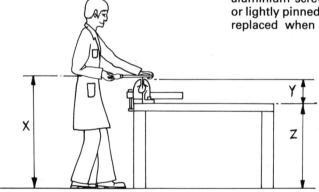

Fig. 1
X = height from floor to elbow
Y = height of vice
Z = height of bench
Height of bench is derived from X-Y when worker is standing upright.

surface itself is then protected and its life increased.

Steel or aluminium angle section screwed around the edges of the bench surface is also a good idea. This helps to stop splintered or 'chewed' edges developing and may be used when making long folds.

Mallets

One process that is very much associated with sheet metalworking is hammering in several of its many forms. Not without reason are professional sheet metalworkers often referred to as 'tin bashers'.

When we want to form metal sheet into various shapes by hitting it, but do not want to mark the surface, then we use a mallet. Mallets can be considered as soft hammers.

There are many types of mallet available that are useful in the working of sheet metal. Some of the more widely used ones are shown in Fig. 2.

To start with, the most generally useful one in my experience is the hide mallet. As its name suggests the head is made from a tightly rolled strip of animal hide. It can be used for most kinds of external work such as folding and forming curves. It is a good general purpose mallet.

The boxwood, or tinman's mallet as I prefer to call it (since several mallets have boxwood heads), can be used for similar work to the hide mallet. However, since it has sharper corners, it is more useful for flattening the bottoms of tray and plate-like shapes. It is also useful for exerting greater pressure than may be obtained by the softer hide mallet when dealing with more resistant metals like mild steel.

One point worth considering by the complete beginner is that if you mis-

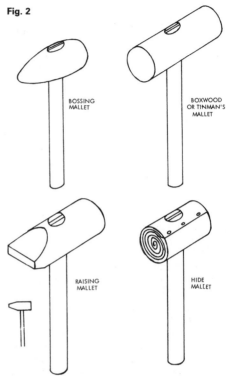

Fig. 2

BOSSING MALLET

BOXWOOD OR TINMAN'S MALLET

RAISING MALLET

HIDE MALLET

takenly hit an edge with a hide mallet little harm results. If you do the same thing with a tinman's mallet, it is quite possible to damage the head. Once the head of such a mallet becomes chipped, or has lumps split off, its usefulness is very much reduced.

The bossing mallet is used when producing concave shapes and should be kept strictly for such work. The radii on either end of the head are essential for it to produce such shapes. They will quickly be damaged if it is used on flat surfaces, for example.

Bossing mallets are also useful when starting to form flanges on circular items.

The raising mallet is the least used of

9

the four, being kept entirely for use when producing raised forms. This process will be covered in detail in the relevant chapter, but generally speaking it means the production of deep circular hollow items.

Raising mallets are often made by reshaping the head of a tinman's mallet.

There are other types of mallet that may be obtained that are not shown. Rubber or composition headed mallets may be used as hide mallets, and are less likely to mark the surface of the softer metals like aluminium and copper. They do, however, give a noticeably softer blow and this can restrict their use. Plastic headed or faced mallets are often sold as substitutes for tinman's, hide and bossing mallets. They probably work satisfactorily but they do not seem to have become very popular. Some are made with interchangeable faces so that one tool will function as two or more different mallets. This may commend itself to the occasional user, but I have never found that combination tools seem to work so well as those made specially for the

work in hand. Also, while I have never owned one, it does not seem that they can be as durable as other types. If, however, only small amounts of work are contemplated, then plastic headed mallets may suit you.

The wooden headed mallets could quite easily be made by somebody with a little ability in woodworking. If you do this, remember to use a close grained hardwood. Box is the correct one to use, but doubtless other types could be made to serve. If making your own please remember that the handles should be made of a resilient material. The commercial ones are made of cane. If handles are not sufficiently resilient and a lot of work is carried out it is possible to set up arthritis in wrists and hands.

Soft faced hammers can be obtained with lead, copper or aluminium heads. These could be useful if working on steel, but they are not essential by any means and I would not recommend their acquisition unless really necessary.

In conclusion, I think the average amateur working at home will find that

Assorted tinsnips, from jewellers' to those capable of cutting quite thick metal sheet.

the vast majority of his sheet work can be carried out with the hide mallet. I would, therefore, recommend the acquisition of this tool first.

Snips

The full name of these is tinman's snips, usually shortened to 'tinsnips'. Do not be misled by the name as they may be used on any thin gauge metal.

There are various sizes available (see photo 1) to suit different sizes of work. Their size is measured by their length and settles both the length of cut that can be taken and the thickness of metal that can be cut. The longer handles give the greater leverage required for cutting thicker metals, but remember all things are relative. Tinsnips are not intended for use on anything other than thin sheet and whilst the exact thickness they will cut largely depends upon the hardness of the metal concerned, I would not recommend their use on material over 18-16 SWG (1-1.5mm). Even these can be hard work, especially in steel.

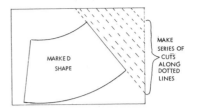

Fig. 4 *Cutting up to an edge with tinsnips to minimise distortion.*

The smallest sizes of tinsnips are usually called jeweller's snips and will be found useful for the small scale modelmaker working with shim-stock.

Apart from size, tinsnips are also supplied as either curved or straight. Straight snips are obviously used for straight cuts, but also for external curves. Curved snips are used for internal curves, although even the smallest ones will not cut very small radii, these having to be filed.

Of the two, the straight variety will find more use in my experience. Ideally, though, both types are required to suit the size of work it is planned to attempt.

Tinsnips are very useful for 'roughing out' shapes in thin material, but they do distort the metal they cut. Mostly, this distortion takes the form of a curve applied to the narrower side of the cut (see Fig. 3). There are ways of avoiding this, such as cutting off thin strips until the edge of the object being cut out is reached (see Fig. 4). Generally speaking, though, where maximum accuracy is required, it is often better to use other methods.

Saws

Most types of saw used in metalworking will find a use at some time for cutting sheet metal.

Fig. 3 *Distortion when cutting with tinsnips.*

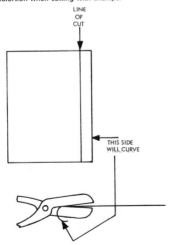

11

FIG.5

Fig. 5 *Backsaw.*

The ordinary hacksaw, if fitted with a fine (32 teeth per inch) blade will cope with metal down to 1mm (18 SWG) but is generally not happy below this thickness.

Junior hacksaws will cope with slightly thinner metal and are useful when short cuts and/or work are the order of the day.

A back saw (Fig. 5) is of much more limited use, but has the ability to produce an accurate straight line cut if used along a surface. It is useful when separating lids from boxes etc, but is probably a tool that most of us manage without.

Not to be confused with the back saw, although very similar to it in appearance, are the razor saws sold by model shops. Although intended for plastic modelling they will cut the softer metals and are useful when cutting straight sided rectangular components, especially from shim stock. Razor saws will probably find most use, from a metalworking point of view, by people who work with metals of shim thicknesses. Small scale railway modelling and strapping for model horse-drawn vehicles are activities which come to mind.

For intricate work in thin sheet metal and shimstock, one of the most useful saws is the piercing saw. It will cope with material from around 2mm thick, or slightly higher, down to quite thin shimstock. Although it cuts fairly slowly, it is capable of cutting out some of the most intricate shapes with no distortion of the metal.

Piercing saws are usually used vertically with the handle downwards, while the work is rested on a slotted table fixed to the bench or held in a vice. The cutting stroke is the downwards one. Therefore the teeth should point towards the handle, which is the opposite way round to the other types of metal cutting saw.

A wide variety of blades is available for piercing saws and care should be taken to obtain the correct type for the work in hand. As with other sawing work the rule to remember is that the thinner the metal the smaller the teeth required on the blade.

Where intricate shapes need to be cut or where thin sheet needs to be cut accurately and without distortion, then I would regard a piercing saw as indispensable. However, if most of your work is going to be things like boilers for miniature steam locos or car body repairs, you probably will not find much use for one.

When using an ordinary hacksaw the depth of the cut is restricted by the frame. If the line to which one is cutting is close enough to one edge, then the blade can be set at 90° to the frame. This will allow cutting to continue. Unfortunately it is often the case that the line of cut is too far from an edge to permit this technique to be used. In this situation, the sheet saw will be found very useful. It may be fitted with ordinary hacksaw blades and the thin frame (see photo) will fit within the thickness of the cut.

Sheet saws are more difficult to control than an ordinary hacksaw but they are very useful when making long cuts in the thicker sizes of metal sheet — say 2mm upwards.

I have always found it helpful when using this saw to start the cut with an ordinary hacksaw and then continue with the sheet saw. Being easier to control, the hacksaw is more likely to give an accurate start to the cut. This then helps to hold the sheet saw on course when cutting continues.

Tension files consist of a holder, rather like a large junior hacksaw frame, and a round section blade. The blade is really a round file. As such it will, therefore cut rather slowly, but it has the advantage of being able to cut in any direction.

Being thicker than a piercing saw blade they will not cope with quite such intricate work, but they do not need to cut their way around a change of direction. It is possible to stop, then cut away again in a different direction without revolving the blade, because it has teeth all the way round.

Tension files, often referred to as Abrafiles, are most useful when cutting curved shapes or holes in the centre of a sheet. A firehole door opening for a model boiler is an example of the type of work which they do quite well. In a situation like this, a small hole needs to be drilled first and the tension file is pushed through then fitted in its frame. Cutting may then proceed around the outline of the hole required. Metal between 0.7mm (20 SWG) and 3mm (⅛″) seems to be the size with which Abrafiles are happiest. There are three types of blade, coarse for the thicker metal, medium and fine.

It is possible to obtain adaptor clips to allow these blades to fit an ordinary hacksaw frame. This is quite a good arrangement if one is only going to have the occasional job to do. Where any large amount of work requiring tension files is contemplated, however, it is probably better to have a proper frame designed to hold them. A tension

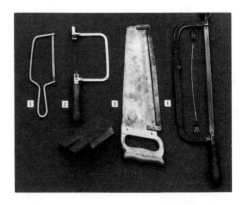

Photo 2 *Illustrated are (1) Junior hacksaw (2) Piercing saw and table (3) Sheet saw and (4) a standard frame hacksaw with tension file.*

file is probably not absolutely essential for a lot of sheet metalwork. I would think, however, that anyone working with sheet metal will have a use for one sooner or later.

There are some mechanical saws on the market that may be used with sheet metal. The most useful is the power jig saw. This type of saw is made by several well known power tool manufacturers, and is most usually advertised as a wood cutting tool. Blades suitable for use on metal may be obtained, however, without much difficulty.

Small power jig saws such as that shown in photo 12 can be used quite successfully on metal up to substantial thicknesses. The thickest material on which I have used one was 6mm (¼″), but they seem to be happiest with the 0.7mm to 4mm range.

Where a lot of sawing has to be done and where cuts have to be made across large sheets, jig saws can save a lot of hard work. In the absence of a sheet saw I have known a jig saw to be the only way of making a particular cut in

13

heavy sheet. They will also cut gentle curves.

Power tools are, of necessity, more expensive items of equipment to acquire and on this basis a power jig saw may be thought of as an extravagance.

Bearing in mind my comments in the previous paragraph, though, I would think that anyone carrying out more than small amounts of sheet metalwork could be well-advised to consider the eventual purchase of such a tool.

A more recent development has been with small bench mounted saws with blades working vertically like the one in photo 3. There are several different makes of these but most of them seem to mimic the action of a piercing saw and take similar kinds of blades. They can be quite useful, if much work involving the cutting out of intricate or curved shapes is contemplated.

Many people now appear to have a small bandsaw as a part of their home workshop equipment. Again, these are usually seen as a woodworking tool, but metal cutting blades can be obtained. If someone owns a bandsaw and is considering working with sheet metal, then it is probably worth obtaining some metal cutting blades. I would not think a bandsaw to be a tool worth obtaining just for cutting sheet metal, however.

To conclude this section on saws, it must be repeated that the saws needed to work sheet metal depend upon the type of work to be undertaken.

The hacksaw and junior hacksaw are sufficiently useful to be considered practically indispensable. The others will be either useful or essential when carrying out the type of work for which they are designed. Personally, I have found that to cope with the sheet metalworking arising from general household jobs, car repairs, small scale railway modelling and some model engineering the following saws have proved necessary:-

1. Hacksaw and junior hacksaw.

2. Abrafile blades plus adaptors for the hacksaw frame.

3. Piercing saw for thin/small/complicated shape components.

4. Power hand-held jig saw with metal cutting blades to take the donkey work out of long cuts. This is also useful in situations where a sheet saw would, otherwise, need to be used.

With saws, as with other tools, I have found it a good idea to buy the less frequently used ones when a job occurs that requires them. In this way, a good tool kit is eventually built up without the requirement for a large financial outlay. Also it ensures that one does not spend one's hard-earned money on tools that are not used.

Chisels

Here, of course, I am talking about the tools often known as cold chisels, not the woodworker's variety. Most people will have used these, or seen them used, at some time for cutting concrete, brick and like materials. However, it is not always appreciated that they are also an important metalworking tool. Indeed, their name, 'cold chisel' arises from the fact that they are intended for use on cold metal. Yes, hot chisels do exist, but are much less common, the difference being that they are not hardened and tempered.

A surprising number of occasions will be found for the use of cold chisels in general purpose metalworking. Fig. 6 will, I hope give an idea of some of the types of work for which they will prove useful

When reading textbooks which give details of cold chisels one often finds several different types, or shapes, described. Each is useful for a particular

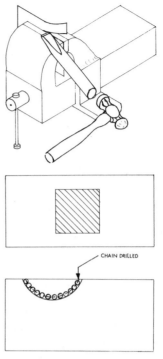

CHAIN DRILLED

Fig. 6 *Examples of cold chisel work.*

type of work. For sheet metalwork, however, the flat or 'ordinary' type, in various sizes, is really the only one required. Chisels for the type of work described in this book should be ground to the shape shown in Fig. 7.

Cold chisels are useful for cutting out holes in the central areas of metal sheets and cutting out chain drilled sections. They are specially useful for this kind of work in the thicker sizes of material.

With thinner material a cold chisel can cut directly without the need for chain drilling, especially if working from an edge. To avoid bending and distortion, it is best if the metal is first placed

15

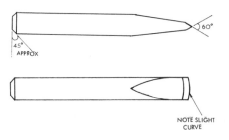

Fig. 7 *Cold chisel suitable for use on sheet metal.*

on a chipping block. This can be any substantial block of mild steel or cast iron with a reasonably flat surface. Placed on the bench, it supports the metal underneath where the cut is being made. Some vices have small anvils cast in which could be used for this purpose, but do not be tempted to use the slide of a standard bench vice. Damage will almost certainly result.

Sheet of around 0.7mm to 2mm (20-14 SWG) can be held in the vice and cut with a chisel as shown in Fig. 6. This technique is often described in textbooks about metalwork. Although occasionally useful, the part not held in the vice will be considerably distorted whilst the part that is held in the vice, although remaining flat, is given quite a heavy burr.

Cold chisels are fairly easy to obtain in tool shops and are not a terribly expensive item. However, the smaller sizes, which are of more use in sheet metalwork, are not always so easily obtained. Also, the hardening and tempering on many bought chisels is rather suspect. For these reasons I have always preferred to make my own. They are not difficult to make. Providing a suitable grade steel is used and care is taken with the heat treatment, home

made cold chisels will work as well as any commercially made ones.

Steel for making cold chisels can often be obtained from good quality tool shops or model engineer's suppliers. Special octagonal section 'chisel steel' is produced but round 'silver' steel will probably be more easily obtained by most people. It is usually supplied in 330mm (13") lengths. The diameter should be from 10mm to 12mm (⅜" to ½") and the length from 100mm to 200mm (4" to 8") to suit the user's size of hand. Hacksaws and files can quite happily be used to do the shaping, although if you are able, forging and filing are better.

The cutting end of a chisel must be hardened and tempered. For hardening, it must be heated to a full red heat and cooled quickly (quenched) in tepid water (silver steel) or oil ('chisel' steel). It must then be cleaned and tempered by again heating the cutting end, but this time only until a purple oxide colour is *just* reached, and then quenched in water.

If broken pieces of mechanical hacksaw blade can be obtained these may be shaped into quite successful cold chisels by grinding. Chisels made in this way have the advantage for the home worker that heat treatment is not necessary. They are also very useful when cutting out chain-drilled shapes because, being thin, they distort the metal less.

One word of warning about cold chisels, and, indeed, all other tools which are hit by hammers, such as centre punches etc. The end which is hit, because it is not hardened, tends to be swelled and burred over by the hammer. Eventually, if this 'mushrooming', as it is known, becomes bad, pieces can chip off during use. These can form quite an eye hazard. Therefore, any mushrooming should be filed away before it gets to the stage of being a danger in this way.

Files

Standard engineer's files in a selection of lengths and shapes are required for working sheet metal. As with other tools, many of these can be purchased as the work occurs for which they are required.

Files are classified by their length, shape and cut (tooth size). They are fairly expensive items, so it is worthwhile choosing the smallest selection that will cover the widest possible range of work. As a general rule, the shape to be filed will set the shape of file to use, while the size of work will decide the length. The grade of cut is partly decided by the amount of metal to be removed and partly by the finish required.

To start with I would recommend the shape of file known as hand and that known as half round in both 150mm (6") and 250mm (10") lengths. The larger files should be of the grade of cut known as bastard and the smaller ones known as smooth.

Additionally, 200mm (8") round and triangular files, both second cut grade, should permit a wide range of filing work. Other files can then be added as the need arises.

It is possible to reduce the cost of acquiring files by buying regenerated (refurbished) files. These are quite satisfactory in use and can be obtained much more cheaply than new files. The only disadvantage is that one often has to buy a selection of shapes, many of which may not find a lot of use.

Standard engineer's files usually require the fitting of a wooden handle, although some are now made with plastic handles moulded on. Do not be tempted to use a file without a handle. The pointed tang can easily be driven into the palm of the hand causing a nasty wound. It is not worth running this risk just to save the cost, or the trouble, of fitting a wooden file handle.

To prevent handles splitting, file tangs should be heated gently and burned into wooden handles.

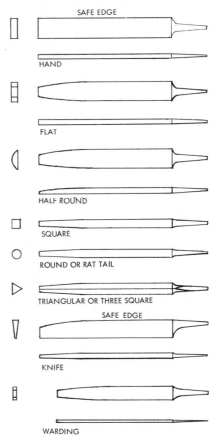

Fig. 8 Engineer's files.

17

For small work and very thin sheet, needle files will be found very useful, probably essential. They are available in a much larger range of shapes than engineer's files and may be obtained in lengths from 100mm to 150mm (4″ to 6″). They are much thinner than engineer's files and can be obtained in sets (at a price!) or individually.

If starting off, I would recommend the purchase of a similar range of shapes to the engineer's files previously mentioned. However, a knife section needle file will probably prove very useful in addition to these. Remember, however, they are intended for small work and will not be of much use beyond this.

All files should be stored when out of use so that they do not knock against each other. They are, of necessity, very hard and, therefore, also brittle and easily damaged by rough treatment.

Bench Shears
These are large bench mounted pieces of equipment that have a similar cutting action to tinsnips. There are various different sizes, but a common commercial one has blades about 250mm (10″) long operated by a handle about 1000mm (3ft) long.

Many of my comments about snips apply to bench shears with the difference that they will cope with thicker metals and longer cuts. The size des-

cribed in the previous paragraph will cope with sheet up to 3mm (⅛″) thickness and cut thicker material than that with an effort.

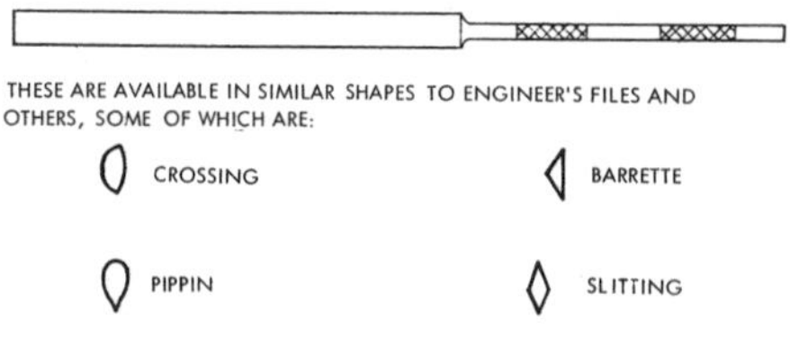

Bench shears are useful for the rough preliminary cutting out of shapes and for making long cuts across large sheets. With the exception of limits imposed by surrounding workshop obstacles (vices, walls etc) they can make an unlimited length of cut, the metal being fed past and beyond the blades as cutting proceeds. With the exception of industrial-type powered machinery, bench shears are probably the quickest and easiest way of cutting out large items. Fitted with a simple length stop, they can also be used to cut large numbers of identical pieces.

Distortion, especially curving, is quite a problem with bench shears, however, and they are not good for precision work nor for cutting thin strips. These will either take on a clock spring or a half ellipse shape.

Bench shears are a fairly expensive item and are not really a priority for the average home worker. As time goes by, however, if the chance of a set comes along, they are probably worth acquiring. A damaged or badly worn set obtained cheaply on the secondhand market could probably be satisfactorily refurbished with simple tools. On the other hand, at least one design for a small set of shears has been published in *Model Engineer*. The one I recall was by L. Brandon and appeared in the issue for 2nd July 1982. It used old files as the blades.

One problem with tools like bench shears in the average home workshop is a lack of space. Normal practice is to have them permanently bolted to the bench but this can restrict the amount of bench space available for other work,

THESE ARE AVAILABLE IN SIMILAR SHAPES TO ENGINEER'S FILES AND OTHERS, SOME OF WHICH ARE:

CROSSING   BARRETTE

PIPPIN   SLITTING

Fig. 9 *Needle files.*

unless one is fortunate enough to have a large workshop. For the amateur working at home, it is probably a better idea to store the shears out of the way when they are not being used. When required they can be clamped to the bench with 'G' cramps. Alternatively, they could probably be held in one of the currently popular portable work benches like the Black and Decker 'Workmate' when needed. This would also have the advantage of allowing large sheets of metal to be handled out of doors, where there is probably more space than in the workshop.

One type of shear that has been developed during the last ten years or so works by cutting a slot through the metal with more of a punching than a shearing action. This has the advantage that the metal is not distorted, especially when cutting thin strips. It is also useful for notching out corners when making boxes. However, I have found this type less easy to control because the metal is more difficult to steer as cutting proceeds. Also they are more wasteful of metal than the traditional shear because of the slot which they cut. This is approximately 3mm (⅛") wide.

Stakes
Stakes are used when forming sheet metal into various different shapes. They are normally heavily made in mild steel, commercial ones often being produced by drop forging. The metal is worked over them with the aid of hammers or mallets, and as a general rule the shape of stake should be selected to match the shape which it is desired to produce. Their surface should be polished or any blemishes will be transferred to the work.

Photo 5 *Typical bench shears suitable for cutting sheet metal.*

A typical range of shapes in which stakes are commercially available is shown in Fig. 10. By no means will the amateur working at home need a full range or even a good selection, unless a large amount of work is contemplated. I would advise acquiring them as the work at hand requires.

So long as it is possible to obtain suitable size steel most people will probably manage to make the stakes they require. For shaping work in softer metals hard wood blocks can be a good substitute for stakes.

Stakes are essential when planishing (Chapter 4) and useful for finishing shapes, especially in harder metals like mild steel and nickel silver.

In use, stakes can normally be held in an ordinary bench vice. Commercially made ones are produced with tapered square shanks that will also permit them to fit into a specially made bench

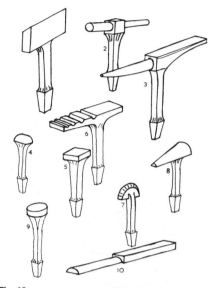

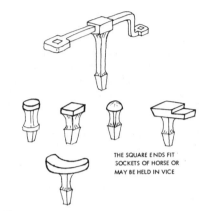

THE SQUARE ENDS FIT SOCKETS OF HORSE OR MAY BE HELD IN VICE

Fig. 11 *Tinman's horse and selection of heads.*

Fig. 10 *A selection of stakes. 1, Hatchet. 2, Side or pipe. 3, Bick iron. 4, Oval head. 5, Square. 6, Creasing iron. 7, Half moon. 8, Funnel. 9, Round bottom. 10, Bench mandrel.*

socket, often steel lined, or into a tinman's horse (see Fig. 11).

Hammers

Fig. 12 shows the types of hammer that are used in the various aspects of sheet metalworking.

Of them all, the essential one to begin with is the ball pein (also seen as pane, peen, or pean) hammer. This can be regarded as the most generally useful hammer to any metalworker. Not for nothing is it often called an engineer's hammer.

The flat face will cope with general purpose hammering. The rounded ball pein can be used for riveting or for hollowing in place of the doming or blocking hammer.

The other hammers shown are only needed if the particular work for which they are designed is in progress. Ob-

viously some are more specialised than others.

A planishing hammer is needed for beaten copper and brasswork that is intended to be polished. A welder's chipping hammer is needed to knock the slag off electric welds on steel.

The tucking hammer is for 'tucking' in wired edges and the raising, doming and sinking hammers are used for the work described by their names. They (the last three) are used when the work is too resistant to respond to a mallet.

If suitable sized pieces of steel can be obtained, it is possible to make one's own hammers, especially of the types that are only needed occasionally. Ideally, hammer heads should be made of high carbon steel hardened and tempered to dark straw, but for a small amount of home use case hardened mild steel heads can be quite satisfactory. However, with the normal range of home heating equipment, I often think that straight hardening and tempering is the easier of the two processes to perform. Welder's and tucking hammers are perhaps the easiest types for home construction as they are often only

20

needed in small sizes.

Hammer handles should be made of ash or hickory. Ash is quite easy to obtain in the size needed for hammer handles, since it grows in many hedgerows and on railway embankments! Metal handles can also be used, but should be given some kind of resilient grip. Commercial hammer handles are not a very expensive item and with normal care have quite a reasonable life.

Hammer heads are usually held on wooden handles by means of a wooden wedge expanding the end of the handle. These can work loose from time to time and need knocking in further to tighten them. Do not neglect to do this as hammers with loose heads are very dangerous items.

Drills

Holes for sheet metalwork are often made by methods other than drilling, especially if they are of large size. A standard jobber's range of drills, in either inch or metric sizes, will nevertheless prove useful. If they are to be used in any form of power tool or on harder metals, like stainless steel, they should be made from high speed steel. Carbon steel drills, whilst cheaper, will just not hold a cutting edge if they get hot because the temper will be drawn.

The larger drills, say over 8mm (5/16") diameter, will not work very well with thin metal. This is because the point breaks through before the full diameter has started to cut. At best, this leads to badly shaped and inaccurate holes. At worst, if used in a machine, to the dangerous situation where the metal is grabbed by the drill and spun round. Many of us have scars which bear testimony to this fact. One way to reduce this tendency is to re-grind the drill to a much flatter angle than that with which it is originally made.

One result of the problems associated with drilling larger size holes in metal has been that various specialist drilling type tools have been developed over the years.

Cook's cutters are hand operated tools that will cut larger size holes in sheet metal of 16mm (5/8") diameter and upwards.

A fairly recent development is the conecut drill (photo 6). This tapered drill is used like an ordinary twist drill, except the different shape of the cutting edges avoids the problems associated with the use of twist drills in thin material. One simply keeps drilling with it until the hole has reached the desired diameter. Having this marked on the metal with dividers before starting will

Fig. 12 *Hammers. 1, Ball pein. 2, Planishing. 3, Peining or tucking. 4, Raising. 5, Welder's chipping. 6, Doming. 7, Sinking.*

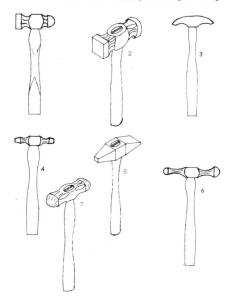

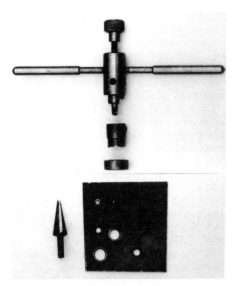

Photos 6 *Top, Cook's cutter for large diameter holes in thin sheet. The cutter and die are at the bottom. The knurled handle exerts pressure via a screw thread and the T-handle turns the cutter. Lower photo shows a 'Conecut' drill for thin sheet.*

help to indicate when the drill has penetrated sufficiently. The tapered edges given to the hole are not serious when working with the thin sheet metal for which the tool is designed.

Since writing the previous paragraph, another type of drill has come on the market, which, in my opinion, is even better for this work than the Conecut. This is the step drill (not illustrated). It consists of a series of steps which range, in the smallest examples, from 4mm to 13mm (5/32" to ½") diameter. It will start drilling into a centre punch mark and when it breaks through the metal it will have produced a hole of the smallest diameter. Further drilling with it will enlarge the hole, (1mm at a time) in a series of steps. These can be clearly 'felt' through the handle of the drilling machine. It possesses, therefore, two

advantages over the Conecut. One is that it produces a parallel-sided hole. The second is that it is very much easier to judge the diameter reached by counting the steps as they break through the metal.

If any amount of drilling is going to be carried out, it is well worth, if possible, investing in a small grinder. Some quite good ones, suitable for home use, are available now, and it is surprising how often drills need re-sharpening.

Punches
Because of the difficulties associated with drilling, larger holes in thin sheet metal are often punched instead.

Numerous types of commercial punches are obtainable, some of which are suitable for the home user in the form known as chassis punches. These can often be obtained from suppliers of motor car tools. Usually they are in two main parts, a punch and a die. They are closed by a draw bolt that passes through a hole drilled in the metal sheet. Such punches will typically produce holes between 20mm (¾") and 50mm (2") diameter.

Another reason for using punches is that square or rectangular holes may be quickly produced.

It is quite possible for the home user to make punches to suit the work in hand. Two parts are required, a male punch and a female die. Again, silver steel or black finish high carbon steel are the metals to use, being hardened and tempered after construction. For soft metals or the amount of use such tools have in the home workshop, case hardened mild steel can be used. Fig. 13 shows two punches that I have made and used in the past. Number one was made when a number of 11mm diameter holes needed to be produced in

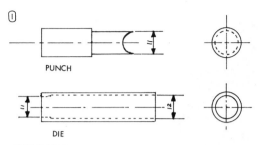

① PUNCH

DIE

BOTH SILVER STEEL, HARDENED AND TEMPERED TO STRAW

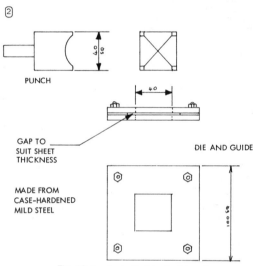

② PUNCH

GAP TO
SUIT SHEET
THICKNESS

DIE AND GUIDE

MADE FROM
CASE-HARDENED
MILD STEEL

Fig. 13 *Punches for tinplate, aluminium etc.*

tinplate. Usually the punch is held in a lathe chuck and the die in the tailstock. The tinplate is placed between them and the tailstock feed screw applies the operating pressure. It could also be used in a drill press or a vice, although the absence of a guide for the punch might make alignment with the die awkward.

Number two was made when a large number of 40mm (1½") square holes had to be produced in 1mm (18 SWG) aluminium alloy sheet. It is normally used by pressing together the punch and die in a bench vice. The guide aligns punch and die and the metal slides in the gap between. The punch is shaped so that the corners pierce the metal first, then the curved sides cut with a shearing action against the edges of the die. Originally it was intended for use in a drilling machine, but

23

Photo 7 *Tank cutter in use, turned with a carpenter's brace.*

Usually, holesaws are designed to cut one size hole only, but it is possible to obtain ones with a number of blades of different diameters. It is then a matter of selecting the blade to suit the diameter of the hole required.

Holesaws are useful if a number of holes of one diameter need to be made. The very cheap ones that are available are, in my experience, best avoided because the blades do not seem to last very long.

Tank Cutter

Photo 7 also shows a tank cutter. This is another rotary tool for cutting larger diameter holes. Unlike the holesaw it is adjustable as to the exact diameter that it cuts.

Tank cutters can be obtained, or made, for use in power tools with a suitable low speed. Often, however, they are made, like the one illustrated, with square shanks for holding in a carpenter's swing brace. They tend to be cheaper than holesaws, whose use is much the same, and can be home-made. Hand powered ones are quite hard work to use.

If this type of work is only done occasionally, a tank cutter may be a better

it was found that the greater pressure exerted by the vice was required.

For punching holes in, or shapes from, shimstock, only a punch may be used with no die. The sheet is laid on a lead block and the punch is hammered into the surface to produce the hole or shape required. This method will, of course, only work with thin or soft material and for small size punches.

Punches are items that can obviously be made or obtained as the work requires. Having said that, like most other tools obtained for one particular job they tend to come in handy on many subsequent occasions.

Holesaws

A holesaw is intended for use in a power drill running at low speed and is used for producing round holes in the larger sizes. Such tools are often used when cutting a hole in a hot water tank in a house to take an electric immersion heater.

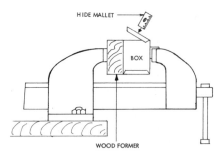

Fig. 14 *Folding the fourth side of a small box around a wood former.*

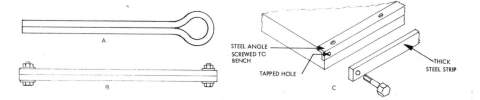

Fig. 15 *Folding Bars. A, commercially made. B, type suitable for home construction. C, bench-edge type for long folds.*

buy than a holesaw because of its adjustable radius of cut. However, it is, in my opinion, inferior to a holesaw.

Blocks and Formers

It is not possible to go into a great deal of detail about these here as different ones could well be required for every item made. They are usually made up to suit the work at hand from hard wood, steel or wood faced with steel.

One of the simplest situations where a wood block can be used is for the production of small hollowed forms. A depression the size and shape of the finished form is gouged out of the wood and sanded smooth. The softened metal disc, or blank, is then shaped by beating it into the depression with a bossing mallet or doming hammer.

A typical use for a former is when folding the fourth side of a box. The first three sides can be formed by folding in the vice or folding bars, but the last cannot be done this way. When working by hand a common method is to make a steel or hardwood block to the inside dimensions of the box but rather deeper. The part-finished box is placed around the former and the two are held together in the vice. This allows the last side to be bent over. Fig. 14 should make this clear.

Many model engineers will come up against the need for formers when making model boilers. These usually require flanges on the end plates/tube plates etc. and formers are required to allow these flanges to be knocked over. Such formers need to be the shape required less twice the thickness of metal being used.

After cutting to shape and annealing, the metal block is then clamped in the vice with the former. The flange can then be knocked over the edges of the former with a mallet.

Any close grained hardwood can be used to make these blocks and formers. Mahogany seems to be the easiest hardwood to buy at the present time and many varieties of it are suitable for this work. Beech is another good one and can sometimes be obtained from old furniture. Soft woods are best avoided but can be pressed into use for the softer metals or for a one-off job. Alternatively, soft wood faced with steel sheet can work perfectly satisfactorily.

Solid mild steel can make very good and durable flanging and forming blocks but it can be hard work shaping it in the thicknesses required. Mild steel is, therefore, usually only used when working with harder metals or when the formers are likely to receive a lot of use.

Folding bars

These are holding or clamping devices for use when making straight line folds

25

in sheet metal. In their simplest form they can be considered as extensions to the vice jaws.

Work requiring to be folded is placed between the folding bars, lined up and then pushed over by hand or knocked with a mallet.

The length of work that can be folded in this way is restricted to the length of the folding bars. Usually they are not made more than about 300mm (1ft) long.

A way of having a longer set of folding bars is to build them into the edge of the bench as shown in Fig. 15.

It is important to remember that folding bars should be made of reasonably substantial mild steel. A thickness of 6mm to 8mm (¼" to ⁵⁄₁₆") is about right.

Heating Equipment and Soldering Irons
For most work with tinplate, and much work with copper and brass, soft soldering will be required. Some form of soldering iron is, therefore, essential for this work.

Although there are now some very heavy duty electric soldering irons on the market, I still believe that the best type for general purpose sheet metalwork is the externally heated type. Corrosive liquid fluxes are often the best

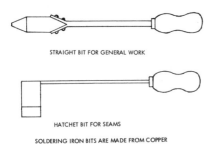

STRAIGHT BIT FOR GENERAL WORK

HATCHET BIT FOR SEAMS

SOLDERING IRON BITS ARE MADE FROM COPPER

Fig. 16 *Soldering irons.*

for this kind of work, yet it is not a good idea to have them around electric soldering irons. Also, the greater amount of heat required to deal with large sheets of metal can better be obtained from externally heated soldering irons.

Proper gas stoves can be obtained for use with externally heated irons but are not really necessary. A domestic gas stove can work just as well, as can a blowlamp or, my own favourite, a small camping stove.

Externally heated soldering irons can easily be homemade, provided suitably sized blocks of copper can be obtained. They may also be bought. The eventual aim should be to possess a selection as the size and shape should suit the work. Common practice is to work with two irons, one being heated while the other is in use.

Fig. 16 shows the two basic shapes, but others can be made to suit special or awkward jobs.

For much, if not most, bending and shaping work, the metal needs to be in its softest possible condition. The treatment used to achieve this is called annealing. Different metals are annealed in different ways but always heating is involved. It therefore follows that some form of torch or blowlamp will be an early requirement.

Much work can be done with the now rather old-fashioned paraffin blowlamp. At one time this was almost the only heat source for the above-mentioned work available to the home worker. Now, however, we have some improved equipment available to us.

Small gas blowlamps working off canisters of butane gas are a very convenient source of heat. Generally they will reach a similar temperature to the paraffin type and are much quicker and easier to light. They will bring small work to a red heat and can do some silver soldering jobs.

For larger work and for brazing, something larger is really needed.

The ideal equipment here would be a blow torch using mains gas and low pressure air from an electric blower. For most people with home workshops, however, this is not possible, either because of cost, the non-availability of a gas supply in the workshop, or both. Therefore, a better solution is probably a propane torch.

Propane gives higher temperatures than butane and if firebricks are used to contain the heat, a propane torch can bring substantial components to a bright heat without difficulty. Torches working off portable cylinders of propane are available from several different manufacturers at reasonably 'affordable' prices. If a choice can be made between butane or propane gases, propane is the one to go for as it will produce higher temperatures.

There are now some small and economically priced oxy-acetylene sets on the market. Some use compressed gas in cylinders and others rely on chemically produced gases. While useful for brazing work, these give a very restricted area of high temperature heat and are not so useful as a blowlamp type of torch for general heating work. They should, therefore, be given a lower priority when acquiring workshop equipment.

This really concludes the chapter about the tools and equipment necessary for the majority of home sheet metalwork. Throughout, I have tried to make clear what can be done without and what is essential for a start to be made. Many of the tools, like hammers and files, will probably already be owned, and it is surprising what can be done with very basic equipment.

To anyone starting from scratch with only the usual household tools, I would say 'have a go'. As skill and experience increase, you will be able to form your own idea of the direction in which your work is likely to go. This will then decide the equipment you will want to obtain in order to produce better and more ambitious work.

CHAPTER 2

Metals and their Characteristics

Metal is considered to be in sheet form when its width and length are very much greater than its thickness. Most of the well known, and some of the less well known, metals can be obtained in this form.

Very thin sheet metal, commonly between 5 and 20 thousandths of an inch thick, is known as shim, or shimstock, and is usually supplied in a package giving a selection of thicknesses. It is greatly favoured by the people who scratchbuild small scale model locomotives. There are, however, many other uses for shim. Copper, brass, nickel-silver and steel seem to be the easiest metals to obtain in this form.

Until metrication, the thickness of wire and sheet metal was described most frequently by the British Standard Wire Gauge (S.W.G.). Now it is simply described by its thickness in millimetres, or fractions of a millimetre. Often under the metric system, units are not stated when a millimetre dimension is given, just the figure being quoted. For example, 0.7mm thick sheet will often be specified as '.7 thick'.

Many people still find the S.W.G. numbers more meaningful, so I have tried to give both figures whenever a thickness dimension is given in this book. The problem is that S.W.G. thicknesses do not come out at exact millimetre dimensions but true metric sheet is produced in reasonably round figures such as 2, 1.5, 1, 0.7mm etc. When quoting thicknesses in the text I have tried to give the nearest common S.W.G. number to the common metric thickness quoted. Suppliers, or their catalogues, are usually quite helpful, fortunately, and will give advice to customers where problems arise. A comparison table of S.W.G. thicknesses and their exact millimetre equivalents is given at the end of the book.

At the time of writing, much non-ferrous sheet is still produced in the old Imperial (S.W.G.) sizes. Sometimes these are quoted in catalogues as exact metric equivalents, giving some very odd figures.

Tinplate
This metal has been one of those most closely associated with general sheet metalwork for a very long time. With the use of plastic mouldings for things like funnels, boxes and toys, its use has declined somewhat during the last 30 years. It is still quite widely used, how-

ever, and most people will have come across it being used to make containers for tinned foods.

Tinplate is not really one metal, but two. It consists of a very thin sheet of mild steel covered on both sides with a layer of tin. By this means we obtain a metal that has the strength of steel but with much better corrosion resistance. It is available in four thicknesses which were, formerly, known as 'X' sizes. Thus 1X at 0.38mm is the thinnest, followed by 2X (or XX) at 0.43mm, 3X at 0.48mm and 4X at 0.54mm.

As a material it has much to recommend it for home use.

It is available in smallish size sheets, typically 712 x 508mm (2' 4" x 1' 8"), which are easily handled. Snips and shears, because it is thin, will cut it with ease. For the same reason it is easy to bend, fold and curve. The steel which it contains also means that it is comparatively strong for its thickness, while it will not rust as rapidly as untreated mild steel.

Tinplate can be riveted and bolted, but for many purposes it is best joined by soft soldering. It is very suitable for this. Again, because of its thickness, it may also be easily joined by folding the edges of the joint over each other to form seams.

When using and storing tinplate it must be remembered that methods must be employed which will not scratch away the tin coating. If this happens, rusting can very quickly follow. Except where they are going to be cut or filed to, lines should not be marked using a scriber. A pencil is the traditional method of marking out on tinplate, but felt tip markers and chinagraph pencils may also be used.

Cut edges, when the steel will have become exposed, should be protected by running a thin layer of soft solder along them. This is known as tinning.

Finished articles made from tinplate may be further protected by paint or varnish. It takes paint with no problems, so long as the surface is clean and free from grease.

Except for soft soldering, tinplate should not be allowed to undergo any process involving the use of heat. Tin has a fairly low melting point and if heated above this the tin coating will be removed. Therefore, annealing and hard soldering processes are definitely out.

Tinplate may be bought relatively easily, but a very useful source of supply is to save old food tins and oil cans, especially the 5 litre (1 gallon) type. These usually seem to use the thinnest size of tinplate, but much work can be done with this. Some cans, especially those containing drinks, are often made of aluminium. As this has very different working properties to tinplate it is important not to get the two types confused. The best check is to use a magnet, which will cling to tinplate (because of the steel) but not to the aluminium.

In view of the sources of supply named in the previous paragraph, tinplate is a very good material with which to make one's first attempts at sheet metalwork. Also, of course, it may be worked with the simplest and most basic of equipment.

Copper

Copper appears to be one of the earliest metals used by man. In the form of sheet it has been in use at least since Old Testament times. It melts at approximately 1083°C.

The price of copper seems to vary rather, but it is generally regarded as a fairly expensive metal. It is commonly available in 1200 x 600mm (4 x 2ft) size sheets in a wide range of the standard thicknesses. Partly because of its cost, copper is not widely used in general purpose work, and so is not often easily available in scrap form.

Better quality kettles are often made from chromium plated copper and an old discarded one could give a supply of thin sheet. For small work thin sheet copper can be obtained by slitting, annealing and flattening copper tube as used in domestic plumbing. Offcuts of this may often be obtained cheaply. For work of any size, however, such as a boiler for a model steam engine, it must usually be a case of buying new material.

Copper is a very nice metal to use when bending, hollowing and so forth as it is very soft and pliable. Malleable is the normal term used in metalworking. It is annealed by heating to red hot and either cooling in water or leaving to cool slowly. If much previous forming work has been carried out, though, it is better to leave it to cool in air to avoid the risk of distortion that rapid cooling can cause.

Filing, drilling, sawing and machining are not so easy where copper is concerned. Being rather soft it tends to tear and clog the tools. Files quickly become pinned, or clogged with shavings, for example. Pinning can be reduced by rubbing chalk into the file before starting, but frequent cleaning will still be necessary. Machine processes and drilling need plenty of oil.

Copper is the best conductor of heat and electricity out of the metals in common use. Many items are made of copper for this reason alone, but it can cause problems. When brazing or soldering copper it will respond quite

well but will need a lot more heating than other metals because of this good conductivity. The heat tends to spread right through the copper, even if it is only applied at one point, and much pre-heating is needed for all but the smallest work. To overcome this problem when hard soldering thicker sheet, it is usual to pack the work with firebricks or coke to help retain the heat, while using a secondary torch, or blowlamp, to heat the body of the work. The main torch is then directed at the joint to bring it to a suitable temperature to melt the solder or spelter. Where the nature of the job will not permit packing as described above, it can be surrounded by firebricks to reflect escaping heat back towards the work. This is especially necessary if trying to attain the higher temperatures needed when brazing.

Copper is very resistant to corrosion by the atmosphere once it has acquired a coating of its bright green oxide. One often sees this where it has been used for cladding on the roofs of important public buildings. It would be too expensive for the average 'semi' though! This corrosion resistance can make it useful for many applications but it should be remembered that some chemicals and salt atmosphere can attack copper. It is also worth noting that it can form a poison when it comes into contact with some food salts. Copper saucepans are tinned or plated on the inside for this reason.

The pleasant red/brown colour of copper and its ability to polish well make it popular for much decorative work.

Because of its cost, work with copper is probably best saved until some practical experience has been gained. Once one is able to mark out and form with reasonably predictable accuracy, however, it can be a pleasant metal to use for some sheet work.

Brass

Brass is an alloy of copper and zinc with a characteristic yellow colour. It polishes, solders and machines well and is a little harder than copper.

It needs to be remembered that the name brass applies to a whole group of copper/zinc alloys. Their characteristics are varied by varying the proportions of copper and zinc. Most of them melt around the 900°C-950°C mark, which means a good red heat in practical terms. Caution is, therefore, required when carrying out heating operations if the work is not to be melted.

The type of brass most likely to be used by the amateur working at home is standard or basis brass. This is suitable for simple cold working and contains 63% copper.

Gilding metal is another type of brass that may well be encountered. This contains 85% copper and is more suitable for beaten work as it is more malleable. Increasing the copper content of brass increases its ability to be used for pressing, forming, raising, etc.

The pleasant appearance of brass and its ability to polish well make it popular for decorative work. Indeed, it is considered almost to be a crime by many people to finish brass or copper articles by anything other than polishing.

On a more practical level, brass is very resistant to corrosion, especially by sea water. It is, therefore, much favoured for items used on boats. Acids can, however, seriously attack it, especially the zinc content.

Like all metals, brass work-hardens when bent and beaten into shape. During the production of an item of this kind, frequent annealing is therefore required. Here, care is needed during heating because of the low melting point. The normal method is to heat the brass until just below red heat and then leave it to cool in air. Quenching can be used, but again, one must take into account the risk of distorting a partly made workpiece.

The correct temperature may be judged by heating until the effect is obtained where different colours appear to be 'flashing' across the surface of the brass in the wake of the torch flame. This is easy to notice but difficult to describe. It occurs just below the temperature at which a dull red colour in subdued light is reached.

Brass is noticeably more expensive than copper, size for size, sometimes considerably more. In sheet form it may usually be obtained in 1200 x 600mm (4 x 2ft) sheets in a range of the standard thicknesses.

As bar and strip, scrap brass may often be obtained from redundant electrical equipment (terminals, plug pins, etc) but it is less easy to find in sheet form.

The amateur is most likely to need to work with brass sheet in the following situations: car radiator repairs, decorative items like spoons, tankards, vases etc, water tanks and bodywork for model locomotives, decorative nameplates and labels, etched model kits. Its use can, also, often be encountered in old or antique tools and furniture. Many chrome plated items are made of brass.

Mild Steel

This is a very useful metal, often neglected by the amateur for sheet work. It does, however, have much to recommend its use.

Like all other steels, mild steel is an

alloy of iron and carbon. Probably for this reason it is sometimes mistakenly called sheet iron.

Because so many items, from office furniture to car bodies, are made from mild steel sheet it is fairly easy to obtain cheaply in the form of scrap. Even if buying new material it is relatively cheap when compared to the non-ferrous (non iron-containing) metals like copper and brass.

Mild steel can be worked by all the normal metalworking techniques with comparative ease. It is not as soft as copper or brass for forming beaten shapes and flanges, often requiring steel rather than wood formers. However, it will work in this way, and is much stronger than many other metals.

Welding, especially with equipment likely to be used in home workshops, is quite easy with mild steel. Where sheet material is concerned, though, distortion can be quite a problem.

To anneal mild steel it needs to be heated to red hot and allowed to cool slowly – the slower the better. For true annealing to take place it needs to be buried in hot coke, sand, ashes etc. to reduce the speed of cooling as much as possible and give maximum softness. Leaving it to cool in air will not achieve such a great amount of softening and is termed 'normalising'. However, for most cold working of mild steel I have found this to be sufficient. Although not really relevant here, it is worth remembering that the higher carbon steels after hardening by heat treatment can be annealed in the same way as mild steel. There is little risk of melting mild steel unless using welding equipment.

The major problem with mild steel is the speed with which it will rust. Bright finish steel will do this much more rapidly than black finish. The oxide coating on black mild steel gives it some protection in this respect. Even if stored under quite favourable conditions (warm, dry atmosphere) mild steel can rust unless coated with oil, grease etc. Rusting also seems to take place more quickly along the lines of any welded joints.

It is, therefore, essential to remember that anything made of mild steel will normally need to be given some protection. There are a number of alternatives.

The easiest method must, undoubtedly, be painting. It is also the most frequently used method and is especially suitable for home use. Good quality paints are easily available and, if used correctly, are quite effective.

Plastic coating and galvanising are other methods giving a more durable finish, but at greater cost and inconvenience.

Mild steel is so very widely used that it is pointless to try to list all the situations where it is likely to be encountered by the home metalworker. In sheet form it finds many uses in model engineering in the form of body sheeting for traction engines, locomotives and such like. Anyone repairing car bodywork is most likely to be working on or with it, as is anybody making or mending machine belt guards and drip trays. Tool boxes, shelf brackets, repair plates and shelving are other things commonly made from sheet mild steel.

As a material I have often found mild steel sheet is overlooked by the amateur worker on account of the rust problem. One often sees descriptions of model locomotives where footplating and cab side sheets and so on are made of brass. I am not advocating its use for water tanks and the like, but where it can be adequately protected by painting or will stay oily, mild steel forms a strong, more reasonably priced alternative. If properly treated and cared for, it can have a perfectly adequate lifespan.

Galvanised Steel

This is mild steel sheet covered with a layer of zinc to protect it against rusting. In concept, it is the same idea as tinplate, but the zinc is a much more effective rust protection. Its appearance is the colour of zinc, silver-grey, but with a very noticeable mottled effect caused by the large grains of which the zinc is composed.

Many of my remarks concerning working mild steel sheet apply to galvanised sheet, except that it must not be heated above the melting point of the zinc (419°C). This means that annealing, hard soldering and welding are out.

Galvanised sheet is most usually available in the thinner sizes like 0.7mm to 2mm (20 SWG to 14 SWG). It is not so easy to obtain from the usual suppliers of materials for amateur use. Probably the best method is to find a local engineering firm who are prepared to sell offcuts.

I have not found it easy to obtain galvanised steel from scrap articles. However, I well remember how, in the hard-up days of owning my first car, I cut up an old galvanised bath to do some patching around a headlamp.

Riveting, seaming and soft soldering are the usual joining methods to use with galvanised steel. Cut edges should be tinned, as with tinplate, and heavy scribed lines avoided.

Galvanised steel sheet is a good material to use in situations where uncoated mild steel would be rather prone to rusting. It is a good material for repairing car bodywork, if obtainable, and can be used to make cans, funnels and such like for use with water. In the form of corrugated sheet ('corrugated iron'), much stiffer than flat sheet, it could be used to build your workshop. It can also be useful for outdoor brackets and fittings for guttering and greenhouse shelving. Finally, it can be used in place of mild steel sheet, to give greater rust protection, or to avoid the need for painting. It may be painted in the usual way, however.

Sometimes it is possible to obtain galvanised steel in small sheets, about 600mm (2ft) square, that have been plastic coated on one side. The colour seems to be either black or brown. This material is very useful for making an attractive front surface on switch and control panels.

If working with galvanised sheet it must be remembered that cold working with hand tools cannot be carried on so long as with uncoated sheet. This is because once work hardened it cannot be annealed without melting off the zinc. This not only spoils the material; zinc fumes are a health hazard.

Nickel-silver

In spite of its name, this metal contains no silver, being an alloy of copper, zinc and nickel. Its appearance is probably best described as 'yellow/silver'. At one time it was known as 'German silver'.

Nickel silver may be given varying characteristics by varying the proportions of its constituent metals. Generally, though, it can be accepted as being a strong malleable and corrosion resistant metal. It can be soft or hard soldered, beaten and pressed to shape, machined, drilled, folded, riveted, sawn and filed with comparative ease. Harder than metals like brass, copper and aluminium, it takes a little more effort when being hand worked, but nothing excessive. In sheet form it may be obtained as shim and up to 3mm (10 SWG) thick.

The melting point of nickel-silver is between 1050°C and 1110°C. It is annealed by heating to between 600°C and 750°C, a good red heat, and leaving to cool. Do not overdo the heating, though, as a propane torch could melt the metal.

The only real drawbacks of nickel-silver are that it does not take paint so well and it is rather expensive.

In the thinner sizes, nickel-silver is quite widely used in small scale modelling, especially of railways. Reflectors in oil lamps, torches and older car headlamps are often made from it, too. In the home it is frequently used in tableware as electro-plated nickel-silver (E.P.N.S.) and is much harder wearing than genuine silverware.

Nickel-silver can be summed up as a very useful metal which would probably be more widely used were it not such an expensive one.

Monel

This very useful metal deserves to be more widely known. It is an alloy of copper and nickel with small amounts of iron and manganese. It is similar to nickel-silver in appearance, although with a less yellowish colour.

In strength, monel is almost the equal of steel, but it possesses much great resistance to corrosion. It files, drills, hard solders and may be cold worked quite well. It is a less good conductor than copper.

Monel is potentially, therefore, a very useful metal. Unfortunately it is rather expensive and not very easy to obtain in the small quantities usually required by the amateur user. The cost, however, is not so prohibitive as may appear at first sight when compared to steel and copper. Both these metals are often specified in much more substantial thicknesses than would be necessary for monel, steel because of the corrosion factor and copper to give sufficient strength. Therefore, being able to use thinner material, the cost of using monel for a job is noticeably reduced. Last time I bought any monel, admittedly some years ago, it cost roughly half as much again as similar thickness copper. However, if the job has been done with copper, material of at least twice the thickness would have been required.

Annealing is quite straightforward. Heat to bright red and leave to cool in air. There is little danger of melting it with the usual equipment. Melting point is over 1200°C.

Sources of supply, for the amateur worker, need seeking out. Firms making liquid chemical apparatus like dry-cleaning machines, and so on, may be prepared to sell off-cuts. It is sometimes available from surplus suppliers, but is often only obtainable in large quantities from normal non-ferrous metal stockists.

Monel may be found useful in any situation where strength and corrosion resistance are needed. In many ways it is an ideal metal for the outer shells of model steam boilers. Its lower conductivity and greater strength give it an advantage here over copper. Its corrosion resistance gives it the advantage over steel.

Aluminium

This grey/silver coloured metal is best known for being very light in weight and therefore widely used in aircraft construction.

Pure (for practical purposes) aluminium sheet is available, but most so-called aluminium used today is really aluminium alloy. These alloys, and there are many hundreds of them, are made up of copper, manganese, magnesium and aluminium. Compared to pure aluminium, they give a great improvement to strength and machining properties. The name Duralumin is often applied to them, being derived from 'durable aluminium'. Many of them have the ability to harden, or stiffen, with age as well as the more usual work-hardening.

Aluminium and many of its alloys are easily cold worked, being quite malleable after annealing. They are fairly resistant to corrosive attack but not by salt water.

Although easy-to-use solders have come on the market in recent years it is generally considered a difficult metal to solder or weld. Rivets, screws, nuts and bolts and glues are therefore often used for joining it together. Pop rivets can be especially useful when working with it, usually being made of it themselves.

Aluminium is one of the lightest metals and is also a good conductor. It finds many uses because of one or both of these characteristics, often being used in place of copper for electrical conductors.

The amateur worker will often find aluminium useful for making boxes and containers, especially for electrical and electronics gadgets. It may be used to make chassis for these items and heat sinks for transistors and other solid-state devices.

Being fairly easy to obtain in sheet form, aluminium is often a useful metal for general purpose sheet work. Care must, however, be taken in its working and application because it has quite a low melting point, normally about 650°C.

For this reason, annealing requires care. The recommended procedure is to heat it to 400°C and allow to cool in air. With normal equipment the difficulty is knowing when this temperature has been reached. Fortunately we are able to employ a useful little 'dodge' here. Before heating, an ordinary bar of soap is rubbed over the surface of the aluminium, which is then heated until the soap turns black. This indicates that the annealing temperature has been reached, and the work is left to cool in air.

Aluminium, in all its forms, is a fairly easy metal to obtain from scrap components. In sheet form it can be found in all sorts of containers, cooking utensils, camping and photographic equipment, commercial vehicle and some motor car bodywork. From all these items, and many more, useful aluminium sheet is likely to be obtained cheaply, or, even better, free!

New material is not difficult to obtain either. My local tool shop sells off-cuts of around 1ft x 2ft size of 1mm to 2mm thickness and this does not seem to be uncommon practice. Shops selling motor cycle spares, decorating and building materials, and modelling equipment are often found to sell aluminium sheet off-cuts. This is in addition to the more usual metal suppliers.

Cost-wise aluminium seems to work out at about the same as mild steel, size for size. Maybe a little more expensive. Weight for weight, however, it is noticeable more expensive.

Aluminium is quite a good metal to try out in the early stages of one's experience as it is comparatively easy to use. Remember, though, that some of its alloys are age hardening and that if annealed at the end of a working period will quite likely be found to have hardened by the next evening. All things are relative, though, and even in its 'hard' state, aluminium is still quite a soft metal.

The home metalworker is likely to encounter aluminium sheet, in particular, when making or mending any of the items mentioned as scrap sources Additionally sports equipment, model railway controller cases, model and full size aircraft can all have parts made from it.

Do not, however, mix aluminium with steel, if possible, certainly not when wet or damp are likely to be present. They have, under these conditions, a very corrosive effect on each other. Steel bodywork on motor cars should never, for example, be repaired with aluminium patches, or vice versa.

To sum up, then, aluminium is a useful metal to have in our stores at home, provided its characteristics and limitations are not overlooked. Certainly one to try out early in one's career as a sheet metalworker.

Other Metals

Although the metals already described are the ones most likely to be of use in the normal run of home sheet metalworking, there are others which may occasionally be encountered.

Lead is probably best known for being heavy and used on church roofs. It is not always realised that it has been used for roofing work on some quite ordinary buildings. Flat roofs over bay windows of pre-war houses can be found to be lead-covered for example. Some water pipes in older houses can still be found to be of lead as can chimney flashings and valley gutters. It is in these situations, when repair work is needed, that it is most likely to have to be worked with.

From a working point of view lead is very soft, malleable and easy to cut, with a low (327°C) melting point. It will readily bend into quite complicated shapes without annealing. Simple shapes can often be formed by hand pressure alone. It is usually joined by seaming or a welding process using a blowlamp and plumber's solder. I have even seen it welded using an oxy-acetylene torch but this method is definitely only for the experienced worker. It is very corrosion and chemical resistant.

It should be remembered that lead, and especially its dust or fumes, can cause poisoning. Using lead sheet is unlikely to cause dust, but care should be taken to wash the hands well before touching any food when it has been used.

Model railway enthusiasts can find small pieces of lead sheet useful for adding weight to locomotives and rolling stock and it is widely used for ballast in model boats.

Zinc is another metal that may occasionally be encountered in sheet form. Like lead, it may be found used for roofing. It may also be used for corrosion resistant containers. It is not so soft as lead, but may still be cold worked without great difficulty. Soft solder and dilute hydrochloric acid flux may be used for joining it. It melts at 419°C.

Pewter is an alloy of lead and tin that finds some use for making tankards, plates, liquid measures and other articles of a part functional, part decorative kind. It is often used in sheet form and is fairly soft and easy to work. Being harder than lead, it is more durable in use. It may sometimes be encountered in repair work or if called upon to make a presentation piece of some kind like an engraved tankard.

Pewter is a grey colour and will take quite a nice polish. It is usually joined using a special low melting point soft solder. Articles made from it are often engraved to that effect somewhere out of sight, such as under the base.

Sources of Supply

One is often asked 'Where can I buy metal'? Here, therefore are some suggestions. Unlike timber yards, metal stockholders are not usually so easy for the non-professional user to find. They can be found scattered around the country, however, and usually seem to be in the more urban areas or on industrial estates.

In Britain, the 'Yellow Pages' telephone directory and various trade directories are good places to start looking. Some of the more useful suppliers I have used have been found in this way. It is most common to find them listed as ferrous or non-ferrous metal stockholders. Before placing orders, however, it is important to establish the policy of any selected firm over supplying small quantities. Some have minimum orders or small quantity handling charges and many have substantial delivery charges.

If the intended sheet metalwork is in conjunction with a hobby, a bulk order by a club for that hobby can often be a way round this. It is fairly safe to assume that the amount of metal required for most amateur jobs will be considered a small quantity by most stockholders.

It is still possible to find the odd local blacksmith who is willing to sell small quantities of metal to private buyers. Such craftsmen, though, do most of their work with bar and strip steel and may not have much in the way of sheet material.

Many factories working with metal can be persuaded to sell offcuts, especially if they produce largish components when small pieces of sheet are unlikely to be of much use to them. Neighbours who work in such places can often be useful contacts for this purpose.

The individual homeworker interested in model engineering and other similar hobbies will probably be familiar with the magazine *Model Engineer*. There are usually several firms advertising there who will supply small quantities of metal by mail order.

It is possible to do quite a lot of sheet metalwork using material otherwise considered as scrap. Sources of supply in this direction have been mentioned when considering the individual metals. It is wise not to allow anything in the home to be thrown out as junk until it has been checked for useful material!

Two suppliers I have found very useful for small quantities of sheet metal of various kinds are K. R. Whiston Ltd of Stockport, Cheshire, and J. Smith and Sons of Clerkenwell, London. Both advertise in *Model Engineer* and Whistons certainly supply by mail order. I hasten to add that I have no connection with either of these firms, being simply a satisfied customer.

I hope, then that this has helped to dispel the idea that metal is a difficult material for the amateur worker to obtain. It is true that suppliers take a little more searching out than for other materials, but they can be found without a great deal of trouble.

CHAPTER 3

Marking and Cutting

Marking Out

Before cutting and shaping can commence, the shape of the required item must be drawn out on the metal. This process is called marking out.

The basic marking out tool for most metalwork is the scriber. There are many different designs and most toolshops sell at least one. They are also quite easily made from thin silver steel rod. A sharp point, hardened and tempered, and a comfortable length to hold in the hand are the main requirements.

The use of a scriber is to be preferred, if possible, to other methods because it

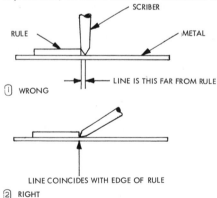

Fig. 17 *How to use a scriber.*

makes a thin and, therefore, accurate, mark that will not rub off. Since it works by scratching marks into the surface of the metal it should not be used on tinplate, and other kinds of coated steel sheet, if the coating must remain intact.

Much marking out work involves drawing straight lines against a rule or straight edge. When doing this, the scriber should be tilted in the way shown in Fig. 17. This helps to put the line accurately in the correct place, which should be hard against the edge of the rule.

To guide the scriber and to measure with the basic tool is the 300mm (1ft) rule. Buy a good one, some cheap ones appear to have the first mark in from the end oversize. Whether it is graduated in millimetres, inches or both is up to personal preference.

When working with larger sheets a steel tape measure will be found useful, as will a long straight edge of 600mm to 1000mm (2ft to 3ft). Long metal straight edges can be expensive to buy but quite acceptable ones can be made from suitably stiff lengths of aluminium extrusion, about 25mm x 12mm (1" x ½") or steel strip 30mm x 6mm (1¼" x ¼") are suitable. These may not be accept-

38

able for the finest precision work, but very little sheet metalwork is of that kind.

For marking lines at 90° to edges, a square of some kind will be required. A 100mm (4″) engineer's try square, sometimes mistakenly called a set square, is the most useful type for work within its size range. Again, buy a good quality one and avoid rough handling or it will not remain square for long.

Combination, or carpenter's, squares will be found useful for larger work and may also be used for drawing lines at 45° to an edge. These consist of a 300mm (1ft) steel rule along which slides a head with 90° and 45° angled faces. They may be adjusted to work outside or inside the angle being measured.

Tinman's or blacksmith's squares can also be useful when marking out on large sheets. These are made in a large 'L' shape from thick steel sheet and are usually graduated in inches or millimetres. They are useful in that they may be laid flat on the metal for setting out

90° angles and do not need to be butted up against an edge like the other types of square. For smaller work, a good substitute is a draughtsman's set square.

For drawing circles and curves, engineer's spring-type dividers are necessary. The two hardened and pointed legs may be set to an accurate distance apart and used like compasses. They may also be used when drawing one line parallel to another, using the method shown in Fig. 18. If working with tinplate, or other coated metals when pencil marking is required, ordinary school-type compasses will be found to be a useful substitute for dividers.

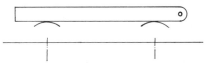

Fig. 18 *Drawing a parallel line. Set dividers to appropriate distance and mark two areas as far apart as possible. Mark second line as shown.*

Odd leg calipers are useful for marking lines parallel to edges. They are especially useful in this way when marking out the width of safe edges in tinplate and allowances for forming wired edges.

Occasionally it is found necessary to draw curves and circles much larger than is possible using dividers. This may be done using trammels. These may be bought, but are another item which can be, and often are, made by the user. In use, one point forms the pivot and the other works around it as a scriber. The bar may be made any suitable length, allowing quite large diameters to be accurately marked.

A centre punch will be needed to mark where any holes are to be drilled. Accurate drilling is unlikely without this preparation.

Light centre punch marks are also useful for locating one leg of dividers or trammels when marking curves.

Dot punches are useful in sheet metalwork, especially when accurate curved shapes need to be cut out. A dot punch is a thinner version of a centre punch, making a smaller mark. Using it, a row of dots can be made along a scribed line. Cutting and filing can then proceed until half of each mark is removed, indicating the correct outline has been reached. Dot punching is also of use when it is necessary to make a fine scribed line stand out more clearly.

A spirit based felt tip pen will also be found useful for labelling parts before assembling and so forth.

When a complicated shape is required, or a number of repeat shapes need to be marked out, a template (or templet) will be found useful. With shapes involving a certain amount of geometrical construction in order to draw them, it is often easier to work on paper to begin with. The shape on the paper can then be cut out to form a template which is placed on the metal and drawn around. There is another advantage to this method. The paper may be bent to shape to check whether it is correct. If necessary it is much cheaper and easier to cut and scrap pieces of paper than pieces of metal. Do not, however, rely on a narrow, curved paper strip, since scissors can stretch the edge being cut and alter the curve.

Paper templates can be glued on to the surface of the metal and cut around, but again, narrow strips can be distorted or expanded by the glue. If something more durable is required, the paper cut-out can be used to make a template of card or even metal. When scribing around these thicker templates remember that, for maximum accuracy, the scriber must be tilted as stated at the start of this chapter.

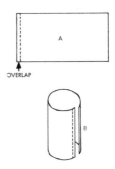

Developments

In sheet metalwork, the term 'development' is given to the flat shape required to produce a three-dimensional object.

Fig. 19 *Forming a parallel cylinder from flat sheet; the simple development at A is rolled to form the cylinder at B.*

This is done by bending and folding the development to produce the item required. Boxes, funnels, small tanks and other containers are produced in this way. It can, therefore, be seen that much marking out consists of drawing developments of the shapes to be produced and some time needs to be spent on the ways in which this may be done.

Some developments are quite simple. They can be 'seen' in the mind's eye and drawn with scriber and steel rule straight away. The development of a parallel sided cylinder, for example, is a simple rectangle. Once the required dimensions are known it may be drawn straight out on the metal, remembering to mark on any allowances for seams, overlaps and edge finishes. After cutting out it may be curved or rolled to shape and the edges joined by whatever method is required. The general idea should be given by Fig. 19.

Developments for rectangular boxes and containers are a little less straightforward but may still be easily drawn straight on to the metal. Sometimes it helps to make a rough dimensional

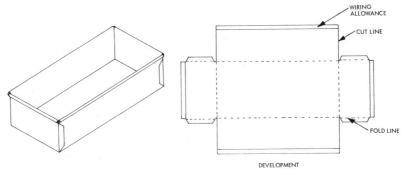

Fig. 20 *Wired edge box with development.*

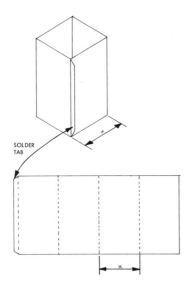

SOLDER
TAB

x

x

Fig. 21 *Development for making a square housing or container. For welding or hard soldering the tab would be omitted and a butt joint used.*

sketch first. Remember to allow any extra metal required, such as for soldering tabs at corners, or for wired edges. Anyone who has made similar items in card at any time will find the shapes required to be the same. Fig. 20 shows a

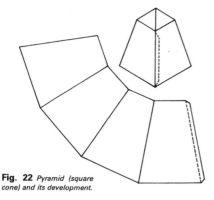

Fig. 22 *Pyramid (square cone) and its development.*

rectangular box, such as might be made for a baking tin or for storing nails, and the development from which it is produced.

Square and rectangular tabular shapes are often needed for containers, boxes, lamp housings and so forth. The development for these items is also a rectangle and may be drawn straight out on the metal.

Any holes required in square and rectangular shapes should be marked out and centre punched on the development. They should be drilled or cut out while the metal is still flat.

When tapered shapes are required, or where the sides of cylindrical objects need other shapes or holes cut in them, the drawing of the development becomes more complicated. It is then best to draw it out on paper with the aid of drawing instruments. The paper may then be cut out and used as a template in the manner already described.

Fortunately, most developments may be drawn with only a basic knowledge of geometry and with quite simple drawing instruments. Ruler, rubber and compasses are the essentials, but a drawing board, tee square and set squares are a big help.

Pyramid shapes, such as a roof for an outside lamp, are, perhaps, the easiest to draw. The idea should be conveyed by Fig. 22.

To draw this development, first draw the one side, obtaining the true lengths of its edges and their angles from the working drawing. Then draw the next abutting it, and so on, until all four sides have been drawn. Lastly, put in any soldering or riveting tabs as required. Whether or not these are needed depends on the exact nature of the job. If it is made from tinplate then they will be needed, also if it is aluminium, for

42

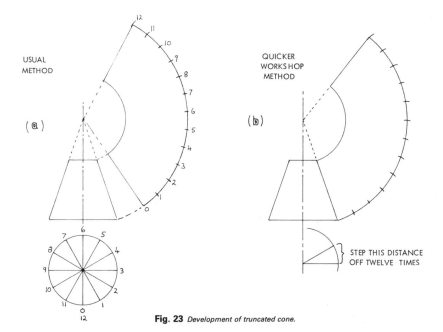

Fig. 23 *Development of truncated cone.*

rivets. Thicker brass, copper or mild steel sheet could have a satisfactory butt joint produced at one corner by hard soldering or welding.

Once the development has been drawn it may be cut out and folded up to check against the job for size and shape. Any necessary alterations may then be made. When all is well, place it on the metal to draw around it.

It may be seen that pyramid shapes with any number of sides may be drawn by this method.

More common, in my experience, are cone shapes. The text book way to draw a development of one of these is shown in Fig. 23. Note that the finished shape required is really a truncated cone, the true cone, which comes to a point, being rarely of use in sheet metalwork. Such developments are required for

many items made from sheet metal, forming a part of many objects that need to be made. Funnels, jugs, tankards, lamp tops and inner firebox sides for vertical boilers are some of the items for which truncated cone shapes are used.

Remember that Fig. 23 shows the TEXT BOOK method. This has been used here because it allows the beginner to see what is happening more clearly. For practical workshop purposes the complete semi-circle under the base does not need to be drawn. One 30° segment of it is all that is required, drawn anywhere convenient. The only purpose of the semi-circle divided into segments is to allow the circumference of the base of the cone to be stepped off with compasses along the base edge of the development. Only

43

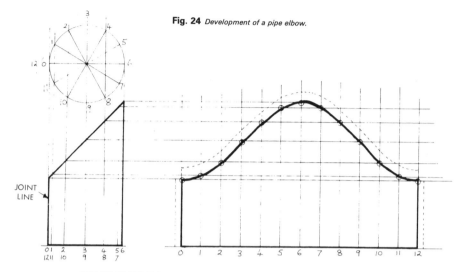

Fig. 24 *Development of a pipe elbow.*

JOINT LINE

OUTLINE OF PIPE AND DEVELOPMENT SHOWN BY THICK LINE.
FLANGING AND SEAMING ALLOWANCES SHOWN BY BROKEN LINES

one segment is, therefore, needed from which to obtain the compass setting. It must be remembered, though, that this distance then needs to be stepped off twelve times to give the correct circumference to the base of the cone. The method is the same, whatever the proportions of the cone, be these long and thin or short and fat. Before cutting out, any additional metal required, such as tabs for soldering or wiring allowances, should be marked onto the development.

Much of the work that requires the drawing of developments involves the shapes that have already been mentioned. Less frequently, other more complicated shapes are required. Fig. 24 shows the development for making a pipe elbow from flat sheet. This has been included because it illustrates well the principle behind the drawing of more complicated developments. This is that the various points around the

shape are obtained from an elevation (side or end view) drawing and transferred across to the development. The points obtained in this way are joined up by a line drawn free hand which then gives the outline of the shape required.

Fig. 25 should further illustrate this principle. It shows a side elevation and development for a traditional metal jug. It could be made from brass, pewter or tinplate, and is made up of two cone shapes and a base. Many items made require a number of different shapes, each needing a different development like this example.

Sometimes items require two different developments drawn together to make them from one piece of sheet. An example of this type is shown in photo 10, which is part of a system for filling a water butt from the run off from a greenhouse roof. The shape of the development from which it was formed is shown alongside. It can be seen that

44

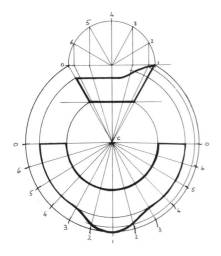

ELEVATION OF COMPLETE JUG.
THE DEVELOPMENT OF THE BASE
WOULD BE THAT OF A TRUNCATED CONE

Fig. 25 *Development of a jug spout.*

it consists of a truncated cone joined to a rectangle. The rectangle folds up to fit around the greenhouse gutter, while the cone fits into a length of water pipe which takes the water to the butt. The device is fixed to the greenhouse gutter with a couple of pop rivets.

Drawing developments can become quite complicated when complex shapes like boat hulls or vehicle body panels are involved. It is probably best, in cases like this, to look up the relevant geometry in specialist publications. However, it is surprising how much may be done with paper shapes cut out and altered by trial and error until the desired development is obtained.

In drawing any development it is a big help to train oneself to 'see' the shape required in the mind's eye first. This comes with practice if the three dimensional object is rolled out flat in the imagination. Making a full size, or scale, drawing of the proposed item before starting work is a good way of doing this. Drawing a simple exploded diagram is also a useful way to help

Photo 10 *Hopper for greenhouse gutter with paper template of development.*

Photo 11 *Battery-operated tail-lamp for 7¼in. gauge train, mostly in tinplate from an old oil can.*

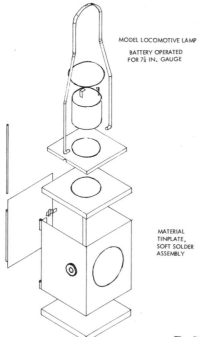

MODEL LOCOMOTIVE LAMP

BATTERY OPERATED
FOR 7¼ IN. GAUGE

MATERIAL
TINPLATE,
SOFT SOLDER
ASSEMBLY

Fig. 26

make decisions over the number of separate parts required. Photo 11 shows a tail lamp made by the author for a 7¼ inch gauge locomotive. The casing was made in tinplate and figure 26 is an exploded diagram, of the type mentioned above, to show the separate parts from which the lamp was made.

Many people with practical interests tend to be impatient where drawing, geometry and planning are concerned. In the case of drawing developments for the construction of sheet metal items it should be realised that it is important to take trouble to get the developed shape right first. Satisfactory construction cannot really proceed until this has been done.

Rectangular Forms

Many of the objects the average home worker needs to make from sheet metal fall into the category of rectangular work. They may not always be true rectangles in the geometric sense but the marking out and cutting procedure is the same. Objects may be, in fact, of square or triangular shape as well.

To give an idea of the way to approach this type of work some typical examples will be described.

Referring back to Fig. 20, the rectangular box is a common shape to have to produce and may occur in many different proportions. Obviously, a square one could be produced the same way.

Fig. 27 illustrates the way in which such a shape could be marked out on the metal with scriber, steel rule and combination square. If working with new metal the corners of the sheet are likely to be square and the development of the box may be marked out from one corner. With out-of-square corners it is best to work from one edge and mark both ends using the square.

Fig. 27

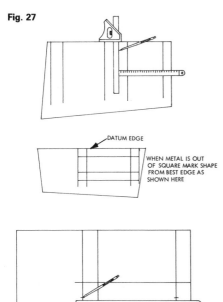

DATUM EDGE

WHEN METAL IS OUT OF SQUARE MARK SHAPE FROM BEST EDGE AS SHOWN HERE

in position, draw the line. Again, this procedure is illustrated in Fig. 25. Lines like these, parallel to an edge, can be drawn with odd leg calipers. When opened out to larger distances, however, these are not easy to use accurately and the above method, using the rule and working to marks, is probably the best way. Odd leg calipers would be quite satisfactory for marking in the allowances for wired or safe edges on a job such as this.

When cutting out this shape (Fig. 27) saw, tinsnips or bench shears should be used, depending on the thickness of the metal and the tools available. It is quite straightforward, the only problem being to cut the internal right angles accurately at the corners. These can be

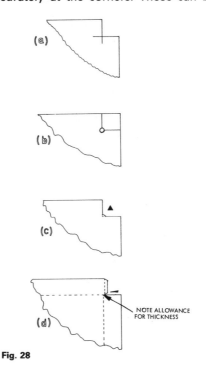

(a)

(b)

(c)

(d)

NOTE ALLOWANCE FOR THICKNESS

Fig. 28

The blade of the square is first set in position. Use the steel rule to push it across the metal until the rule indicates that it is the correct distance from the edge, or line, from which the measurement is being taken. Fig. 27 should make this clear. Once the square is in the correct position the line may be marked onto the metal using scriber or pencil to suit the metal in use. All the cutting and folding lines going across the width of the box can be marked in this way.

To mark the long edges and fold lines, the easiest way is to mark the width on the two furthest apart lines drawn with the square. Place the scriber or pencil on one of these marks and move the rule up to it. Do the same for the other mark. Check back to the first one and when satisfied that the rule is done with snips or shears if care is used, but the danger with this method is that over-cutting can occur (Fig. 28(a)). If the metal is thick enough a saw may be a better method, especially for the beginner.

Fig. 28(b) shows a method that can help to avoid over-cutting as well as giving a neat finish to the corner after filing. This is to drill a small hole of, say, 3mm (⅛″) diameter at the point of the right angle. It is not essential to do this and is sometimes not desirable if, for example, the finished box must be liquid-tight. However, it is one way to avoid the problem illustrated in Fig. 28(a). It can also prevent tearing during folding.

If using saw or snips the cut should stop just short of the inside right angle. The waste metal may then be broken away, the small remaining piece being removed with a triangular file as shown at Fig. 28(c).

Often, rectangular boxes of this kind are made of thin material soft soldered together. For this, flaps, or soldering tabs, are required. This gives an even

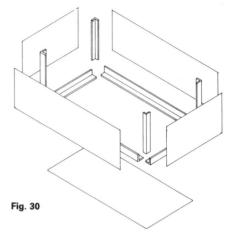

Fig. 30

more acute internal angle to cut. Similar methods to the right angle corners may be employed except that the filing cannot be done with a triangular file. In this case a knife section file should be used (Fig. 28(d)).

Rectangular containers of this kind may be made by other methods. Fig. 29 shows a box made by folding a strip of material, joining it at one corner then adding a base. The sides would be marked out and cut using snips or shears and then folded. The base would then be marked off from the box and cut out by the method described in Figs. 27 and 28. It would then be joined to the sides. This is, perhaps, a better method for deeper items or where folding equipment is limited.

If working with thick sheet, it is better, unless heavy folding equipment is available, to make rectangular items from separate flat sheets joined together at their edges. Joining can be by brazing, welding, or using angle section metal and bolts or rivets. A domestic oil or water storage tank could be made in this way, provided caulking was carried out if rivets or bolts were used. The

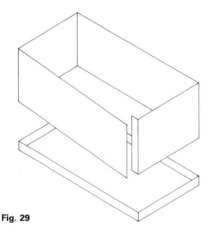

Fig. 29

general idea is shown in Fig. 30, which is an 'exploded' view of such a container.

At the other end of the size scale, a similar method could be used for a water tank on a model steam road or railway locomotive. Here, the rivet construction may well be required for purposes of scale appearance.

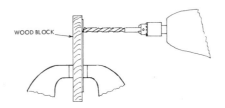

Fig. 32 *Drilling thin sheet in the vice.*

From the point of view of marking and cutting, the procedure is very simple as nothing more than flat rectangles are needed. These may be simply marked out with steel rule, square and scriber before cutting by a method suitable for the thickness involved. That means piercing saw or snips up to 0.7mm to 1mm (20-18 SWG) and shears, hacksaw, jig saw, or sheet saw above that thickness. The angles are simply marked off using square and scriber, then sawn and filed to length.

Fig. 31 shows a heat sink for a transistor which would normally be made from aluminium sheet. Once again, in the flat, this will be a simple rectangle marked out with square, steel rule and scriber. The main point to note is that all the holes should be marked and drilled before folding.

For drilling thin material like this, it is best to hold the metal in mole grips, pliers or hand vice and rest it on a block of wood on a drilling machine table. If using a hand held drill, either electric or hand powered, the set up shown in Fig.

32 will be found to serve most purposes.

As an example of work in the form of a triangle, Fig. 33 is included. This is a small bracket suitable for use when putting up shelves in the workshop. It may be made from aluminium or mild steel sheet up to 2mm (14 SWG) thick. The developed shape is shown at Fig. 33(a) and the finished one at Fig. 33(b). If working with fairly new metal, work from one corner, if not, mark a line at 90° to the best edge near one end. From here, mark the length of the horizontal side with square and scriber, line 1, followed by line 2. Then mark lines 3 and 4 with rule and scriber, or these could be marked with the aid of a draughtsman's or school set square against a previously marked line. Finally join the end of the two fold lines to give line 5, and mark the position of the holes.

The bracket should be cut out as a pure triangle and then the acute corners can be cut off to give the shape re-

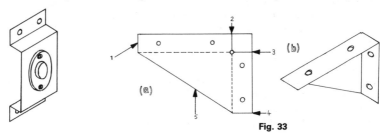

Fig. 31

Fig. 33

49

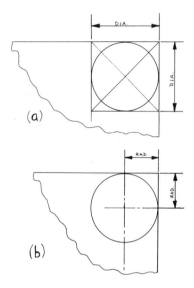

Fig. 34 *Marking a circle from one corner of the metal.*

inside a square whose length of side equals the diameter. If such a square is marked on the metal first, its diagonals will give the centre for marking the circle (Fig. 34(a)).

It is possible to work as in Fig. 34(b) by marking the radii instead, but this has one disadvantage, especially for the inexperienced. When cutting out the disc it is best to start by cutting it out as a square. If the method in Fig. 34(b) is used, it is quite easy to cut too near to the corner and cut into the marked disc. At best, a difficult time will be had trying to curve the cut back on its

quired. Centre punching and drilling of the holes follows and the right angle corner may be cut out using the same method as for the rectangular box. After filing and cleaning up, the bracket is ready for folding.

Discs

Round shapes, or discs, often need to be produced for bases or as blanks for hollowing, sinking or raising. They may be drawn on the metal using dividers, or trammels if the radius is large. The centres should be lightly centre punched to locate the point of the dividers or trammels.

Start by marking the centre from which the circle is to be drawn in such a way as to waste as little material as possible. As with much marking out, it is best to work from a corner of the metal, remembering that a circle will fit

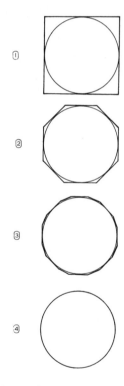

Fig. 35 *Stages in cutting out a disc.*

50

course, with the attendant risk, if using snips or shears, of badly bending the metal. With the method used in Fig. 34(a), whilst there is a little more marking out, there is a line for the cut to follow which can make life easier.

For cutting out and shaping discs it is best to start by cutting them out as an approximate square and then cut the corners off the square. The octagonal shape thus produced can then have its corners cut off, and so on, until a many-sided shape is produced. This is then filed to the marked line. Fig. 35 shows these stages, which may be followed using any cutting method appropriate to the thickness of the metal being used.

If the disc is to have a hole in its centre, and a lathe is available, it may be turned to final size instead of filed. To do this the centre hole is drilled first and then used to bolt the disc to a threaded mandrel held in a three jaw chuck. The speed should be matched to the diameter being turned, which may well mean the slowest available. Light cuts are also the order of the day, especially if the metal used is thin. Plywood discs can be bolted on behind very thin metal to give the necessary support.

Slots

These features can prove puzzling for the inexperienced worker to produce as there often seems to be no way to get cutting tools to inside edges. The exact method used depends upon the size and proportions of the slot.

Fig. 36 shows a variety of forms in which slots can be encountered and the ways in which they may be cut out.

At (a), where the width is at, or near, a drill diameter a hole may be drilled at the bottom. A cut down either side re-

moves most of the metal and files will then do the cleaning up. In narrow, parallel slots like this, a warding file is the one to use.

The wider slot shown in (b) may be produced in either of the ways illustrated. If the material is thin, a saw or snips may be used to make cuts in the order shown by the left hand drawing. The triangular shaped piece left may be filed, broken or chiselled away and all edges filed to finish them. This will work with up to 1.5mm (16 SWG) thick metal.

With metal above this size, the method used in the right hand drawing will be easier to use. There, a line of holes has been drilled along the bottom of the slot close to each other and to the edge of the slot (Chain drilling). This should be done first, then a saw cut

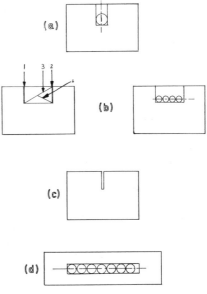

Fig. 36 *Slots.*

51

down either side will allow all the metal in the slot to be removed by chiselling. Make sure the piece being removed is not pointing at anyone's face when nearing the end of the cut. It can fly out as the chisel breaks through. To avoid this, the last small piece may be bent backwards and forwards to break it away. This method could also be used if the bottom of the slot was curved.

An alternative method is to cut all round with a tension file, or piercing saw. With thin material this method may sometimes be quicker but both these saws cut rather slowly when the metal is of any thickness. It is then, usually, quicker and easier to use a hacksaw or to spend time marking and drilling holes.

Very narrow slots, like that drawn at (c), are sometimes needed. If they are 3mm wide or less, they can be produced with an ordinary hacksaw. Two saw cuts right beside each other can be made. However, this is not very easy and a better technique is to mount two or three blades in the hacksaw at the same time, to give a wider cut in one go. Usually, it is not possible to fit in more than three blades at a time and this restricts the width of slot it is possible to cut in this way. In practice this is not much of a problem, because once this width has been reached we are up to the size at which a drill can be used at the bottom of the slot as at (a).

Where a slot has to be cut within the central area of the metal the method shown at (d) is the best approach. It may be used for slots up to about 6mm to 8mm (¼" to ⁵⁄₁₆") if ordinary twist drills are used. Where cone cut type drills are available it is possible to go larger. After drilling, chisel or tension file and files may be used to finish the slot to shape.

Although the slots which we need to produce can come in many shapes and sizes, it will be found that most come into one of the classes described here. It is, therefore, possible, with a little ingenuity, to adapt the methods shown to a wide variety of work.

Large holes

Ordinary round holes in sheet metal, where they are fairly small, are no problem. They can be drilled in the usual way. Larger holes, and holes that are shapes other than round, are the ones that need special treatment.

The maximum size of hole that may be made with an ordinary twist drill varies according to the thickness of the metal. With shim material it is often not possible to drill a 3mm (⅛") diameter hole without tearing the metal or getting an oval hole. With 3mm thick metal it is usually possible to drill holes successfully up to 12mm (½") diameter and perhaps larger. Most sheet metal used in general purpose home work is more likely to be around 0.7mm to 1mm (20-18 SWG) thick. Here 6mm to 8mm (¼" to ⁵⁄₁₆") must be regarded as the largest size drilled hole possible.

The cone cut drills, already mentioned, are a way of going above these sizes in metal up to 2mm (14 SWG) thick. They may be obtained in diameters up to 41mm (1⅝").

Large holes in thin sheet material are, therefore, normally made by punching, sawing, chiselling or filing. Commercially, punching is very widely used and in mass production work it gives a very quick way of making large numbers of holes. Punches are quite straightforward to make and two designs suitable for home construction are given in the chapter about tools. They are not especially difficult to make, but do take up some time and so are probably not justified unless a number of holes of the same size and shape need to be made. For one-offs and small numbers of holes it is better to use one of the following methods.

If the outside shape of the hole is marked out first, a small hole can be drilled to allow a tension file or piercing saw blade to be passed through the metal. The hole can then be sawn around. This method will cope with any holes in thin metal quite well.

For thicker metal it is probably quicker and easier to chain-drill around the inside of the hole and remove the metal with a cold chisel. It would also be possible to cut from hole to hole with a tension file.

In both cases the hole is finished to size and shape with files.

Chiselling

Chisels and the situations in which they are of use have been mentioned several times already, so their usefulness in sheet metalwork should by now be clear. They are of use in many awkward situations where cuts need to be made within the area of a piece of sheet metal. Cutting along the bottoms of slots and the edges of holes are two examples of their use that have already been described.

The 'text book' use of a cold chisel shown in Fig. 6, Chapter 1, shearing metal held in the vice, although useful, is infrequently required. Their greatest use, in the writer's experience, is for cutting out metal after chain drilling has taken place. When this is being done the work should be rested flat on a chipping block with the chisel held vertically. It is best to cut half way through from one side, then turn the work over and cut through from the other side.

This helps to reduce the danger of the cut piece flying out. Not much of a hazard when cutting out holes, but it is when removing metal from slots. In that case, it is best to make sure that the material being removed is pointing away from faces of anyone present, including the worker. It is usually possible to leave the piece being removed just hanging on and break it off to avoid this problem.

Heavy cast iron bench chipping blocks may be bought, but they are rather expensive items and it is probably better to obtain an offcut of thick mild steel plate. A piece about 150mm (6") square and between 10mm and 20mm (⅜" to ¾") thick should be suitable although smaller pieces can be made to serve. Chipping blocks can also be used as a useful bench anvil for many kinds of hammering work, such as riveting and centre punching.

Small cold chisels are best for the kind of work described here. The larger types, as used for brick and stone cutting, are rather too cumbersome to be used for cutting accurately to a line. They also take too long a cut at one go. Between 100mm and 150mm (4" to 6") is about the right length and 10mm to 12mm (⅜" to ½") the width. Cutting edges should be kept sharp, being finished on an oil stone after grinding, and re-sharpened as soon as they are even slightly dulled.

When removing metal after chain drilling, the standard type of cold chisel can be found to be causing distortion of the metal as a result of its rather thick cutting edge. To avoid this, a thin chisel may be made by grinding a cutting edge on one end of a broken piece of mechanical hacksaw blade. Ordinary hand hacksaw blades are too thin and weak. The width at the end should also be ground to reduce it and the teeth removed or bound with tape to protect the hand. Being thinner, a cold chisel made in this way will cut through a chain drilled piece more cleanly and is less likely to distort the metal because it does not try to force it so far apart as it cuts through.

Chain Drilling

Reference has been made several times in this chapter to the process of chain-drilling, so readers should by now be aware of what is meant by the term. Apart from the uses already mentioned, it is also useful when cutting out shapes whose edges consist of a number of different curves.

A number of points need care if chain-drilling is to be used successfully. Not least of these is the marking out of the positions of the holes. To start with, the size of drill to be used must be decided upon. This is largely influenced by the size of the work, but should not be very small in comparison or the marking out and drilling will take up an excessive amount of time. The aim is to remove the metal along the edges of the feature being cut out, accurately, and in a reasonably short time.

Having chosen the size of drill to be used, the next task is to mark a line, half the drill diameter, away from the outline being worked to. This forms the centre line for the line, or chain, of holes. Sometimes it is advised that this line should be a little more than half the drill diameter away, and if there is a possibility of the drill wandering off, this is a good idea. If a vertical drilling machine (drill press) is being used and pilot holes are drilled before the final size, then it is not difficult to make the edges of the holes just kiss the outline marked. If aiming to leave a gap be-

tween the edge of the drill and the line being worked to, make this gap as small as possible or much unncessary filing will be required.

Once the centre-line of the holes has been marked their spacing can be stepped off along this line with dividers. Set the dividers to the exact diameter of the size drill to be used. Again, advice is sometimes given to space the holes a little further apart than this to avoid the holes running into each other. However, with a little practice, it is possible to make the edges of the holes just touch so that very little work is needed after drilling to remove the metal required. Usually the size of the feature being cut out will not be exactly divisible by the drill diameter so a gap between holes will need to be left somewhere. This must be arranged to suit the work in hand. Sometimes it does not matter where it goes, sometimes it does.

When the positions of all the holes have been marked, they must be centre punched. This is the secret of all accurate drilling to marked lines. Care must be taken to place the point of the centre punch at EXACTLY the point where the divider marks cross the centre line. Do not then try to produce a full size punch mark right away. Instead make a small mark by giving the centre punch a light tap with the hammer, then look at it. If the mark is not exactly where required it may be 'led over' by putting the centre punch back in the mark and pointing it in the direction in which the mark has to be moved. A further light tap with the hammer will move the mark sideways, hopefully to the correct position. If not it can be 'led over' again in the necessary direction until it is where required. Once this position has been achieved put the centre punch back in the mark again, but this time hold it vertically and hit it

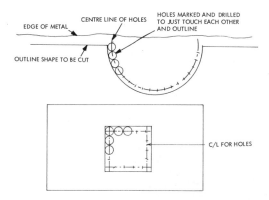

Fig. 37 *Marked out for chain drilling.*

harder to give a deeper mark. This procedure needs to be followed for each place where a hole needs to be drilled. It may sound a bit laborious but it is not really so once a little skill has been acquired in marking out and centre punching. The writing of this description has taken a good deal longer than marking out and centre punching quite a long chain of holes!

After centre punching, the holes may be drilled. Start with a fairly small size drill and follow it with the final size. A small drill is less likely to wander off from the centre punch mark than a large one, which is then almost certain to follow the line taken by the smaller drill. If one hole runs into another and the drill binds, stop and go to the next hole. If two holes are obviously too close together to be successfully opened out to the larger size, leave one of them. These odd small gaps in the line of holes can be cut through with chisel or saw quite easily.

Finally, the metal can be removed with chisel or saw and the outline filed smooth. Fig. 37 shows the ideal situation for which one should aim.

The Tension File and Abrafile

Tension files have been mentioned several times already and so some idea of their use should, by now, have been acquired. These, whether used in their own frame or with adaptors, in a hacksaw frame, are the easiest to use in the writer's experience. Abrafiles can also be had as a more file-like version of this tool. They are round in section and vary from 1.5mm to 6mm (¹⁄₁₆″ to ¼″) diameter. They may be used in the same way as the tension file, but not being held in tension, tend to bend too easily to be convenient in this situation. The fact that they will bend, however, makes them useful for work inside curved items, such as pipe elbows.

The tension file may be used to cut most curved shapes in sheet metal from about 0.7mm (22 SWG) to 2mm (14 SWG) thick. They will cope with a thicker material but tend to become progressively slower and more laborious above 2mm. They may be used like a saw, but remember they will cut in any direction in which pressure is applied, so care is needed in this respect. Also, they do not seem to like being

Photo 12 *Power jigsaw cutting sheet steel clamped to bench.*

overheated and are rather more fragile than hacksaw blades, therefore, cut slowly and let the tension file travel through the metal at its own speed. If cutting downwards, do not let the full weight of the saw frame rest on the blade. A good guide in this respect is that if the tension file is starting to curve noticeably, ease off the pressure. If using a hacksaw frame, take care not to apply too much tension.

When a hole within the area of a workpiece needs to be cut out and a tension file is to be used, a hole must be drilled first to allow the file to be passed through. The size of this is not critical, it just needs to clear the ball shape at the end of the file. A 3mm or 4mm (⅛" or 5⁄32") drill is about right. Pass the tension file through, mount it in the frame, hold the work in the vice and start to cut.

Thin material is rather 'whippy', so keep the place where cutting is being done as close as possible to the vice jaws. Move the work around as often as necessary to keep the cut in this position.

If it is not possible to keep the cut close to the vice jaws, as is often the case with larger work, one hand may hold the metal to give a steadying effect. Alternatively the work may be clamped to the bench with the cut line near to the edge. It is also possible to sandwich the metal between strips of wood positioned slightly to one side of the cut line while it is held in a vice. A portable type work bench, with its long gripping jaws, can also be very useful in this situation.

Using a Jig Saw

Much of the cutting work described in this chapter could, where the metal is greater than .5mm thick (23 SWG upwards) be done with a power jig saw. It is important to ensure that the correct blade is fitted (see instructions on the packet) and that the work is securely held. Photo 12 shows a typical set-up with the metal held down with G-cramps. Their position was selected so that the saw could be held in a good position for photography in this case, so remember that some experimentation may be needed to position them out of the way of the saw for each individual job. Again, strips of wood and the portable work bench can come in useful to hold this sort of work.

Generally, the rate of cut with these saws seems to be rather slow when compared to snips, chisels or hacksaws. They seem to come into their own for making long, or gently curved, cuts across larger sheets or away from edges. They can also prove useful in the case of anyone past his or her prime (is that the polite way to put it?) who lacks the energy for large amounts of hand powered cutting.

Internal Corners
These need to be cut out when making rectangular boxes or any other L-shaped features. Often they are right angles, but may need to be more acute than this, at times. The method used has been described in the section on cutting out rectangular shapes. This may be applied in any situation where internal corners need to be cut out.

Cutting out Strips
Cutting narrow strips from sheet material can present difficulties. Sometimes it is possible to buy thin metal in strip form, but from time to time this is not possible and narrow strips need to be cut from sheet. The difficulty is to cut them in such a way as to prevent the strips curling up or otherwise distorting. Snips and shears are no use, therefore, in this situation.

The tool shown in Fig. 38 is often recommended for this kind of work. It will, if used with care, cut parallel to an edge and make repeat cuts of equal width. Any number of undistorted strips of the same width may be cut by this method. It is quite suitable for home

construction or could be adapted from a carpenter's marking gauge. No dimensions have been given as these will depend on material available and the type of work required.

Alternatively, the cutting blade, which should be hardened and tempered, could be fixed into a simple handle and run along the edge of a rule or straight-edge.

The marking out and cutting procedures outlined in this chapter have been selected with the idea that they cover what have been found to be typical situations. It is hoped that readers will be readily able to see how they may be applied to any particular work that may be in hand. Many jobs will not come neatly into the categories in which work needs to be grouped for constructional descriptions. It is then best to look at the detailed features of the job and decide which type of marking out and cutting problem applies to each. The appropriate method may then be chosen for each section of work. If any job is broken down into a series of small tasks, rather than considered as a general piece of work, it is usually much easier to see how to proceed. This could be written out as a 'plan of campaign', but after a little experience most of us find it possible to visualise the methods in our minds.

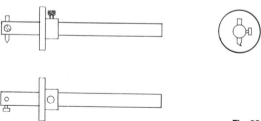

Fig. 38 *Tool for cutting narrow strips from thin sheet.*

CHAPTER 4

Shaping Methods

Before folding or other forming can take place, the metal needs to be in its softest condition. Tinplate and galvanised steel have, of necessity, to be used as supplied. Other metals should be annealed unless they are very thin or the bending and folding work required are of a minimal nature. The annealing method for the metals listed in Chapter 2 are described in that chapter.

The processes described here will include those used in beaten metalwork, which is the term used to describe the

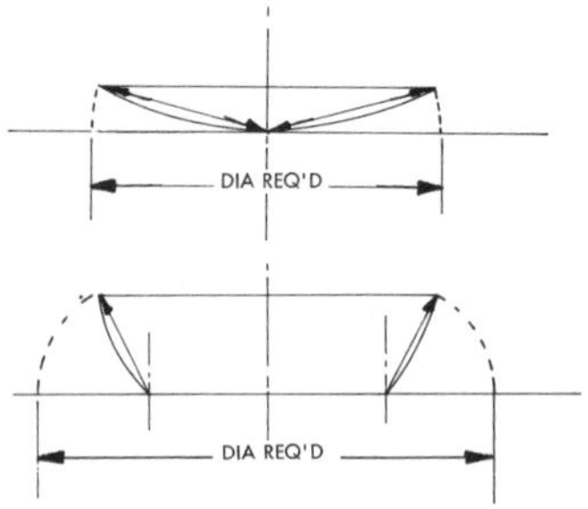

Fig. 39 *Estimating sizes of blanks for hollowing. Differences between straight and curved distances are made up for by the metal stretching during hollowing.*

more decorative and artistic side of sheet metalwork.

Hollowing
This process is used for the production of shallow rounded, dish or bowl shape items. The work starts off as a flat sheet, often, but not always, in the form of a disc, called the blank. The diameter of disc-shaped blanks for hollowing can be worked out by the method shown in Fig. 39.

After cutting and filing to shape the blank is annealed, then hollowing can commence. For softer metals, such as copper or aluminium, a bossing mallet and sandbag are used. Harder metals, like steel, require more force and so a doming hammer or ball pein hammer and wood block may be needed. For small hollowed forms a doming block and punch can be used; these are shown in Fig. 40.

It is best to start hollowing by hitting the blank near its centre and working gradually outwards with concentric rings of mallet or hammer blows. As work nears the edge of the blank, it should be tilted to allow the hammer or mallet to impart a curved shape to the sides. The blank should be moved

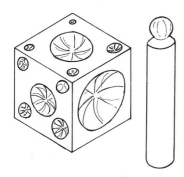

Fig. 40 *Doming block and punch. Punches are available in various sizes to suit depressions in block.*

around under the hammer or mallet to control the shape achieved. Frequent stops should be made to look at the work to see how the shape is progressing.

During forming, the blank will quickly become work-hardened. It is easy to tell when this stage has been reached because the metal feels noticeably more resistant to the hammer or mallet blows. As soon as this condition is reached, anneal the metal again. Do not be tempted to press on because the metal will become increasingly resistant and hard to work. In an extreme case cracking can occur.

The required shape should be produced as nearly as possible. If it is not quite smooth or evenly formed, this will not matter, because after hollowing it can be worked over stakes, and later planished, to tidy up these aspects.

During hollowing, look for high spots or flat areas in the metal. Move it so that they rest over the middle of the sandbag or wood block and knock them down. Vary the force of hammer or mallet blows to match the amount of shaping each is desired to produce.

These are, really, all the rules that can be given with regard to hollowing. Much of it is common sense, and becomes obvious as work proceeds. Certainly, where and how hard to hit the metal become obvious with very little experience. It is quite an easy process to use and a hollowed form can make a good introduction to beaten metalwork.

Sandbags, as their name suggests, are simply strong leather bags full of dry sand. Commercial ones are rather expensive, but it does not require much ingenuity to make a light duty one for home use. About 250mm (10″) diameter is a useful size.

The sand used in commercially made sandbags appears to be of a fairly

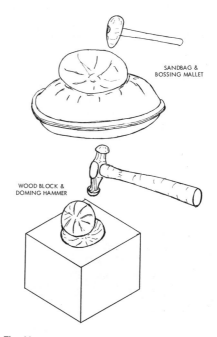

SANDBAG & BOSSING MALLET

WOOD BLOCK & DOMING HAMMER

Fig. 41 *Hollowing.*

Photo 13 *Sandbag, bossing mallet and a copper bowl made by hollowing with them.*

coarse variety, but ordinary builder's sand, if dried, should be perfectly satisfactory.

Apart from the obvious copper bowls (ash tray for the workshop or club-room?) hollowing is useful for making domed end plates for model boilers. It is sometimes known as doming.

Raising

The process of raising is used to make deep circular forms from flat sheets, again usually of a decorative nature. A vase is a typical example of a raised

Photo 14 *Wood blocks for hollowing. 1, pin tray or ashtray. 2, for 2in. candle drip trays. 3, for hollowing the bowl of a small spoon.*

form, as could be a dome cover for a model locomotive.

Raising is more difficult than hollow-ing and is quite time-consuming to carry out. Work needs to proceed gradually, in easy stages, with very fre-quent annealing to keep the metal as soft as possible.

A circular blank is prepared as for hollowing. This is then annealed and is beaten from the outside over a suitably shaped stake. This is shown diagram-matically in Fig. 42. A raising hammer or mallet may be used for this work, but if one is new to the process it is best to start by using a mallet. This is less likely to damage or dent the metal.

When raising, start at the centre of the blank, tilting it, and resting it against the top corner of the stake. Work all round the metal in a circle, then move slightly outwards and work round in another circle. Keep working outwards with concentric circles like this until the outer edge is reached. Anneal, and then repeat the beating process. The aim is to work all over the blank, slightly shap-ing it, then work all over it to shape it a little more. This is continued until the desired shape is obtained. Control may be exerted over the shape being pro-duced by the way the blank is moved over the stake and the spacing of the hammer or mallet blows. It is best to err on the side of insufficient shaping as it is easier to take the work further than to reduce the amount of raising carried out. Flared tops to items may be pro-duced by tilting them the opposite way, with the top edge resting on the stake, and beating a little way back from the edge.

As with hollowing, it soon becomes evident during raising where and how to move and beat the metal. Frequent stops need to be made to view the progress of the work. This is important in deciding where next to beat it, especially when nearing completion. It is also important to proceed slowly, only shaping the blank a small amount at a time. Inexperienced workers can often spoil raised work by trying to alter the shape too much in one go. Apart from this, frequent annealing is the other main requirement. It is sometimes helpful, when making raised forms, to start the shape by hollowing, moving to the raising stake after the shape has been started.

Stakes and hammer faces should be kept clean, smooth, and be well polished. Any slight marks or specks of dust will leave their mark on the surface of the metal. These marks can be detrimental to achieving a good polish later on. Care should be taken over this point during storage of tools.

A wide variety of shapes may be produced by raising and it is surprising how much the metal may be stretched and formed by this process. Caution is required when making deep items, that this stretching does not cause the metal to become unduly thinned as cracking can then occur. If this happens, there is little to be done except to start again. Not good for the temper if much time has already been spent on the work! Fig. 43 depicts a process known as caulking which may be used to progressively thicken the outer edges of articles during raising.

During both hollowing and raising, card templates of the finished shape required will be found to be useful aids. They may be offered up to the work to check the outline when nearing completion.

Apart from specialised crafts like gold and silver smithing, raising is not widely used commercially. Obviously it

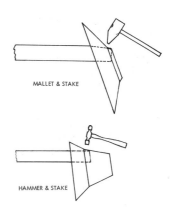

MALLET & STAKE

HAMMER & STAKE

Fig. 42 *Raising.*

would be too expensive, and machine made pressings are often used instead. These cannot, however, reproduce the subtle curved outlines possible with hand raised items, which can result in very attractive and artistic shapes. In spite of this, it is a time-consuming and skilful process. Whilst worthy of use, it is probably better kept in reserve for making decorative items, using other, quicker, methods for those of a purely functional nature.

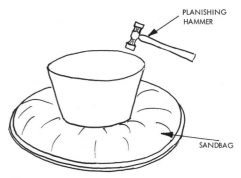

PLANISHING HAMMER

SANDBAG

Fig. 43 *Caulking, a process sometimes used to thicken the edges of items thinned during raising.*

Sinking

This is the last of the three main processes used in the production of decorative beaten metalwork. It is used to make shallow angular sided items, usually with flat bottoms or rims. Plates and trays are typical of the kinds of shapes produced.

The stages in producing a typical item by sinking are shown in Fig. 44. The annealed blank is rested on the stepped wood block with its edge bearing against the two pins. It is then hammered whilst being revolved against the pins. As with other beating processes, it is important not to try to change the shape too much in one go. Slightly form the depression all the way round. Anneal, and then form it a little more all round, and so on.

During this stage, do not expect the rim to stay flat – it won't! Periodically, it will need flattening with a mallet to remove the waves which tend to form as the metal is stretched.

Continue in the way described in the two previous paragraphs, until the desired amount of sinking is achieved. Then the corners may be sharpened up and the rim finally flattened in the way shown in Fig. 44. Finish shaping by flattening the base.

As with the other processes, much work needs to be done by eye, checking the job frequently whilst shaping is carried out. The way the metal responds to the hammer blows will soon become obvious.

When starting, it is a good idea to mark the inner edge of the rim by drawing a circle on the blank in pencil. The pins in the wood block, if hammered in at the correct places, should put the metal in the correct position for the width of rim required. This is not easy to guarantee, however, and the pencil line is a useful guide in the early stages of sinking.

An alternative method of sinking is to turn a depression of suitable depth and diameter into a wood block. The blank may then be annealed and laid over the top of this. Shaping is achieved by using a tinman's mallet to knock the metal into this depression. This should take place in gradual stages as for other work of this kind, with frequent annealing to keep the metal soft. Flatting of rim and bottom can proceed as in Fig. 44.

Folding

Simple right angle folds for box corners and suchlike may be easily produced using folding bars and mallet. Small work may be folded by holding in the vice and knocking round, or by bending with pliers. For folding edges of any length, however, some kind of folding bars will be required. Apart from ones built into the edge of the bench, these are either of the one or two piece kind (see Chapter 1). Any type is satisfactory,

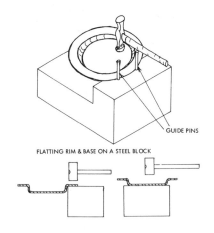

FLATTING RIM & BASE ON A STEEL BLOCK

GUIDE PINS

Fig. 44 *Sinking.*

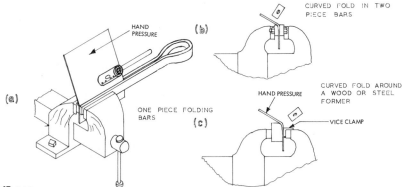

Fig. 45 *Folding.*

but the two piece kind do have the advantage that one corner of one bar may be rounded off to allow radiused bends to be produced. They may also be easily made in the average home workshop. If making folding bars, remember that they should be of substantial thickness material, compared to the metal with which they are to be used.

The normal requirement is to produce a 90° fold. This is first marked on the metal which is then placed in the folding bars and lightly clamped. With one piece bars this is done by gripping in the vice, using just enough pressure to hold everything in place. With two piece bars, tighten the screws and nuts holding them together just enough to give the same effect. The metal is then moved with finger pressure or gentle mallet blows to align it exactly as required and the bars are tightened firmly. Two piece bars should then be clamped in the vice. Hand pressure and mallet blows just above the line of the fold are used to fold the metal to what looks like 90°. It may then be checked with a square and any slight adjustments made until the angle is correct.

Folds greater than 90° may be obtained simply by not working the metal round so far. Simple templates cut from offcuts of tinplate, or other thin sheet or card, to the angle required may be used to check the angle instead of the square. Alternatively, this could be done using a protractor or sliding bevel.

Sharper folds than 90° are started in folding bars in the way described above. After a right angled fold has been achieved, these are then folded further by knocking over a hatchet stake. The metal may be tilted to a greater or lesser degree to obtain the angle required, which may again be checked with card or tinplate gauges, protractor or sliding bevel.

In folding, as with other shaping and forming work, it is important to work in easy stages and not try to produce the fold all in one go. The whole length should be worked first to slightly fold it. Then fold it a little more and a little more until the required angle is reached.

When the fold is well away from an edge, mallet blows alone are insufficient and will tend to impart a reverse curve to the metal (Fig. 47). Pulling the metal over by hand, while hitting at the

63

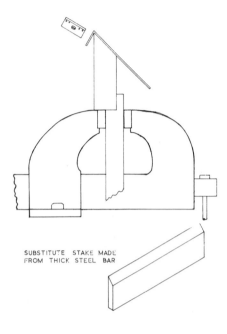

SUBSTITUTE STAKE MADE
FROM THICK STEEL BAR

Fig. 46 *Folding beyond 90° over a hatchet stake.*

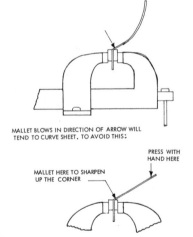

MALLET BLOWS IN DIRECTION OF ARROW WILL
TEND TO CURVE SHEET. TO AVOID THIS:

MALLET HERE TO SHARPEN
UP THE CORNER

PRESS WITH
HAND HERE

Fig. 47

point of the fold with a mallet, is the way to avoid this tendency.

When making safe edges, the metal has to be folded right back on itself. This is not only done for safety reasons, but to stiffen thin metals, like tinplate, when no other edge finish is being used The procedure is to work as for an acute angle fold to less than 90°. When this has been produced on the hatchet stake, the metal is laid flat on the bench block and the edge folded right down with a mallet (Fig. 48).

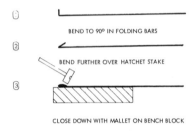

①

BEND TO 90° IN FOLDING BARS

②

BEND FURTHER OVER HATCHET STAKE

③

CLOSE DOWN WITH MALLET ON BENCH BLOCK

Fig. 48 *Safe edge.*

Much folding is carried out for the purpose of making boxed and other rectangular shapes. Figs. 20 and 21 in the previous chapter show the two normal ways in which these are made.

The type made by forming a square tube then adding a bottom is the easiest of the two to fold to shape. One corner at a time is folded using folding bars in the manner shown in Fig. 49.

When the sides and bottom are made from one development the procedure is a little more complicated. The joining tabs are folded first, in folding bars. Then the metal is moved upwards slightly, to allow for the thickness of the tabs, and the end folded, still in the folding bars. Both ends may be folded in this way. To fold the long edges, a wood block is required. This needs to be the same size as the inside width and length of the box and sufficiently longer than the box height to allow it to be held in the vice as shown in Fig. 50(b). The long sides may then be folded over the block by hand pressure at first and then finished by mallet blows in the directions shown by the arrows.

When the size of the work permits, the alternative method shown in Fig. 50(b) will be found useful. Here, the vice jaws clamp the work to the wood block

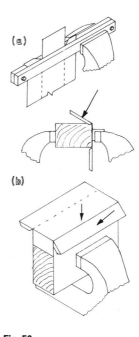

(a)

(b)

Fig. 50

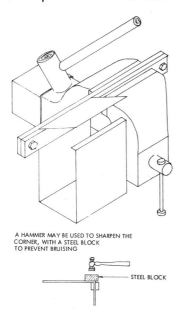

A HAMMER MAY BE USED TO SHARPEN THE CORNER, WITH A STEEL BLOCK TO PREVENT BRUISING

STEEL BLOCK

Fig. 49 *Using folding bars.*

more securely than it may be held by hand pressure alone. This is also useful when dealing with thicker metal.

With a little practice, these hand methods of folding may be used quite accurately and successfully. Their advantage lies in the simplicity of the

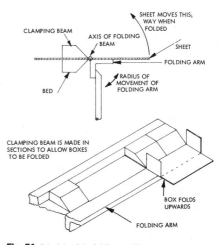

CLAMPING BEAM

SHEET MOVES THIS WAY WHEN FOLDED

AXIS OF FOLDING BEAM

SHEET

FOLDING ARM

RADIUS OF MOVEMENT OF FOLDING ARM

BED

CLAMPING BEAM IS MADE IN SECTIONS TO ALLOW BOXES TO BE FOLDED

BOX FOLDS UPWARDS

FOLDING ARM

Fig. 51 *Principle of the folding machine.*

65

equipment required and they are perfectly adequate for occasional work and when dealing with thin metal. They do, however, become increasingly difficult to use as the thickness of the metal involved increases. For mild steel, 1mm

Photo 16 *Examples of work produced on the above machine.*

(18 SWG) is about the greatest thickness that may be reasonably folded to any great extent by hand methods. Softer metals a little thicker than this can be dealt with, but for the best results, hand folding methods are best kept to thinner material. When thicker material needs to be used, it is better, if possible, to make items up out of flat sheets joined at the edges and keep folding to a minimum.

If folding needs to be carried out with thicker sheet, or if it is desired to take the donkey work out of producing a large number of folds in thinner metal, it may be worth acquiring a small folding machine. Small hand operated ones suitable for use in a larger home workshop are made commercially. These usually work on the principle shown in Fig. 51. The work is clamped to the bed by the clamping beam and the folding beam is rotated upwards about its axis. This is usually operated by a long handle in hand powered machines. Box and pan folders have the clamping beam made up of a number of small sections, or fingers. These may be inserted or removed so that all four sides of a box may be folded.

Right angled folds are often produced industrially by a machine called a press brake. This works in the manner shown by Fig. 52. Press brakes are not home workshop machines, but their principle of operation may be very nearly copied by the use of angle iron and thick square section bar clamped together in a bench vice. If the sheet being folded is placed between the angle and the square bar before clamping, then a fold will be produced. At least one small folding and bending tool of this type, suitable for home construction and use, has been described in *Model Engineer* in recent years. This was in the issue for 5th August 1983, page 144, by A. B. Spiller.

When folding thicker metal, the outer corner of the fold will always take on a small radius rather than a sharp corner. Often this does not matter. Sometimes it does, and then the fold lines need to be gouged out on the inside, to give a vee-shaped groove with a 90° included angle. This groove must go nearly, but not quite, through the metal. The very thin metal at the corner will then fold sharply and the fold can be strengthened and held together with solder. Fig. 53 shows this procedure and a tool for carrying it out. This is made from a piece of silver steel with the end bent over, filed to shape, then hardened and tempered. In use, it is drawn across the metal, which is clamped to the bench, being guided at the start of cutting by a steel rule or straight edge. The file handle should be pinned through, otherwise it may be pulled off during use. The centre line of the groove should follow the centre line of the fold.

This method is normally used when decorative work in non-ferrous metal demands a sharp outer corner. Strap type handles and box corners are examples of work where this process may be required.

Bending

This is a similar process to folding, but produces a curved rather than a sharp corner. The essential requirement is for a former of suitable radius for the required bend.

Bending formers for occasional work need be no more than suitable size round steel bar. This is held in the vice sandwiching the metal to be bent as in Fig. 54(a). Hand pressure is usually suf-

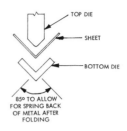

Fig. 52 *Principle of the press brake.*

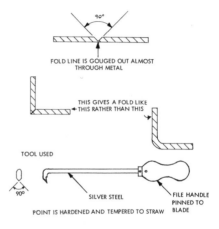

Fig. 53 *Producing sharp folds in thicker sheet.*

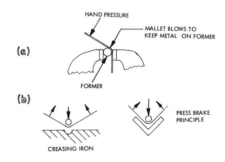

Fig. 54 *Bending.*

ficient to produce the bend, but light mallet or hammer blows may be required to make the metal follow the exact curve of the former. Wire and strips of metal up to the width of the vice jaws may be bent quite well in this way.

A refinement of this method is similar to Fig. 45(c). It can be difficult to align work in the vice when using a round bar-type former. If the bar is not placed below its centre line, it can be forced upwards as the vice is tightened. A length of substantial thickness rectangular bar (6mm/¼" upwards) may have a suitable radius filed on one corner. This may then be used in a similar way to a round bar-type former, with the difference that it is much easier to hold in the vice. As it will be necessary to hold two separate items (work and former) at the same time as tightening the vice, it can be seen that this is an important consideration.

The press-brake principle, already described for folding, may also be used for producing bends. In this case, a curved top-die is used, as shown in Fig. 54(b). This method may be adapted to use simpler equipment. The left hand drawing at 54(b) shows a bend being made by forcing the sheet into a suitable sized groove on a creasing iron by a suitable sized round bar. If no creasing iron is available, a groove may be filed or machined into a block of steel or hard wood for this purpose.

Long edges of boxes, tanks and so forth, will not bend neatly if only held to a former by the width of the vice jaws. To support the work along the whole length of the bend, folding bars are needed. As has already been mentioned, if two piece folding bars are used, the top corner of one bar may be filed to a suitable radius. The metal is then clamped between them and the whole lot held in the vice. Bending may be carried out, as with a simple former, by hand pressure aided by light hammer or mallet blows.

Bends in thicker steel sheet can be made by working with the metal at red heat. A suitable round bar former may be held in the vice so that it sticks out to one side. The line of the bend is marked on the metal and it is heated along this line. Tongs or rags may be needed to allow it to be held in the hands and it is then placed over the former and bent with hand pressure. This is not a very easy task but I have found it useful on odd occasions. Remember that the ordinary engineer's bench vice is usually fitted with hardened jaws, so do not leave the hot metal in place longer than necessary. If the vice jaws become excessively hot, they will be softened.

Bends, as opposed to folds, can be required for a number of purposes. In model engineering work and tank production they can be needed for appearance sake. Remember though, that a bend imparts less stress to metal than a sharp corner and can reduce the possibility of cracks appearing. These are especially likely when bending bright mild steel sheet in line with its grain structure.

Allowances for Bending and Folding
When a piece of metal is bent or folded, the metal on the outside is stretched whilst that on the inside is compressed. The true line of the bend or fold only exists somewhere within the thickness of the metal. This is called the neutral line or plane. An allowance needs to be made for this fact when bending or folding.

Before going further, it must be pointed out that because much home

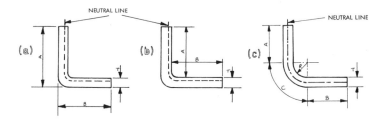

Fig. 55 *Bending allowance.*

sheet metalworking is with thin material, bending allowances may often be ignored. The inaccuracies resulting from ignoring this fact increase as material thickness increases. In my own experience they can be safely ignored for all but the most precise work until a thickness of around 1mm (18 SWG) is reached. Even when bending allowances are needed, if one is not of a mathematical turn of mind it is often possible to work to an acceptable degree of accuracy without them. This is done by allowing extra material either side of the bend or fold line and cutting to size after bending or folding has taken place. Or, bent or folded parts may be made first and other parts marked off from them, rather than being made 'dead' to size.

Thicker sheet and/or really accurate work will require these allowances to be worked out. In these cases, some knowledge of the methods is required.

Figs. 55(a) and (b) show a piece of metal that has been folded to a sharp right angle with the neutral line indicated. The true length of metal required, before folding, is the same length as the neutral line, and has to be found by calculation. The exact position of the neutral line depends upon the type and nature of the metal concerned. For sharp right angle folds in soft steels

and ductile non-ferrous metals, it is 0.2 x thickness from the inside of the fold. For harder metals it is 0.3 x thickness, and for radiused bends it may be taken as half the thickness.

To work out the length of material, if working with soft mild steel, in Fig. 55(a), the procedure is as follows. The outside dimensions are given, but if these are simply added together, the blank will be too long. From each must be deducted the distance of the neutral line from the OUTSIDE of the metal. If this is 0.2 x thickness from the INSIDE of the fold, it follows that it will be 0.8 x thickness from the OUTSIDE of the fold. An amount equal to this (0.8 x thickness), therefore, needs to be deducted from each of the dimensions, A and B, to give the true length of blank required. More simply, 1.6 x thickness (2 x 0.8) may be deducted from the sum of A plus B. Expressed as a formula, the length of blank for Fig. 55(a) may, therefore, be found by A plus B minus (1.6 x T), where T is the thickness of the metal. Millimetres or inches may be used in either fractional or decimal figures, but the same units must be used throughout each calculation. If using a pocket calculator, it will be necessary to work with decimal figures, whatever the units in which one is working.

In Fig. 55(b) the inside dimensions are

given. The bending allowance, in this case, is obtained by adding to A and B the depth of the neutral line below the inner surface of the fold. Therefore, in this case, A plus B plus (0.4 x T) equals length of blank.

Fig. 55(c) shows a radiused bend. Here, the length of arc of the neutral line on the bend (c in diagram) needs to be calculated and added to dimensions A and B. The circumference of a circle may be found by the formula π x diameter. (π equals 3.142). For a 90° bend, the length C will be one quarter of the circumference of the circle of which it is a part. The diameter may be found by adding the inside radius of the bend (R) to 0.5 x metal thickness and multiplying by two (R plus ½T x 2). For other angles, an appropriate length of arc must be calculated.

To use the bending allowance, once it has been calculated, it is necessary to mark and cut out the blank or development to the size required. Mark the length from one edge to the start of the fold or bend. Hold this part in the folding bars or machine and then fold in the normal way. In other words, the bending allowance is applied on the part of the work OUTSIDE the folding bars or clamping beam (Fig. 56).

When using bending allowances, it is best to test the calculations made on scrap material before starting the actual work. Differing equipment and types of metal can cause variations from stand-

ard to occur. A table of bending allowances is given at the end of the book.

Allowances also need to be made for the thickness of the metal used when forming various containers. Two typical examples are shown in Fig. 57. At (a) is our old friend, the rectangular box made from a flat development. The solder or rivet tabs in this case are to go outside the ends. To allow this the fold lines need to be spaced in from those for the tabs by an amount equal to the metal thickness. At (b) the length of side after folding needs to be the length of the box less twice the metal thickness.

Planishing

This is a hammering process normally used at the final stage of shaping dec-

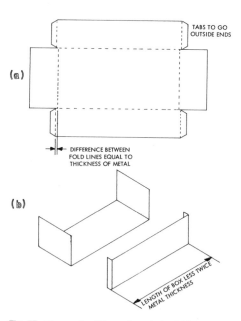

Fig. 57 *Allowance for thickness of metal when folding.*

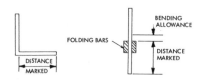

Fig. 56 *Application of bending allowance.*

orative work. It is used with hollowed, sunken or raised shapes as a means of smoothing out the shape. In addition to this, it has two other important functions. These are to compress the metal, and so close its surface pores, and to impart a small amount of work-hardening. Closing the pores gives a more suitable surface for polishing. The work-hardening makes the finished article more durable and resistant to accidental deformation.

Because it produces a pattern of facet-like marks over the surface of the metal, planishing is sometimes used as a method of decoration. In spite of this its main purpose is as described in the previous paragraph.

Before planishing is started, the work should be cleaned thoroughly to remove all traces of oxide, soldering fluxes and so forth. The usual way this is done is to pickle the metal for around ten minutes in a bath of dilute sulphuric acid. Upon removal from the pickle bath, the metal is washed and dried. During washing, it may be scoured with pumice powder or other mild abrasive like 'Vim' or 'Ajax', if further cleaning is necessary.

Good pickle baths can be made from large plastic cake boxes or old car battery cases. Dilute sulphuric acid can sometimes be a problem as chemists are often wary of selling acids to the general public. I have usually obtained mine at home from old car batteries – hobbies do make one into a hoarder! Some model engineering suppliers advertise sulphuric acid, but usually the buyer has to collect it.

If diluting acid it is important to add the acid to the water, not the other way around. Dangerous boiling, fuming and splashing can occur if water is added to acid. For the same reason, hot metal

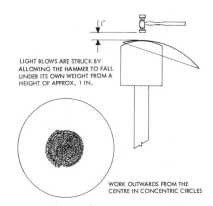

LIGHT BLOWS ARE STRUCK BY ALLOWING THE HAMMER TO FALL UNDER ITS OWN WEIGHT FROM A HEIGHT OF APPROX. 1 IN.

WORK OUTWARDS FROM THE CENTRE IN CONCENTRIC CIRCLES

Fig. 58 *Planishing.*

should not be placed in acid baths. Allow it to cool first.

Fig. 58 shows the essentials of planishing. A suitable stake is selected and the work placed over it. A proper planishing hammer should then be used to lightly tap the work all over its surface. The word 'light' must be stressed, heavy blows should be avoided. Just lift the hammer about one inch from the metal and allow it to fall under its own weight, perhaps with a very gentle flicking movement to help it on its way. The surface should have a barely noticeable mark afterwards, no more. Start in the middle and work outwards in a series of concentric circles until the whole surface has been planished.

During planishing, it is important to ensure that the point of the work where the hammer hits it is resting on the stake. If this is not done, deformation of shape can occur. Also the main effects of planishing are gained as a result of the metal being slightly squeezed between hammer and stake. This is the reason why it is important to start in the centre and work outwards. As the metal is squeezed, it is also slightly expanded.

71

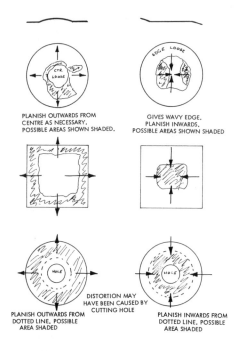

PLANISH OUTWARDS FROM
CENTRE AS NECESSARY.
POSSIBLE AREAS SHOWN SHADED.

GIVES WAVY EDGE.
PLANISH INWARDS.
POSSIBLE AREAS SHOWN SHADED

PLANISH OUTWARDS FROM
DOTTED LINE, POSSIBLE
AREA SHADED

DISTORTION MAY
HAVE BEEN CAUSED BY
CUTTING HOLE

PLANISH INWARDS FROM
DOTTED LINE, POSSIBLE
AREA SHADED

Fig. 59 *Planishing to remove distortion.*

During planishing the surface finish of hammer and stake is reproduced on the metal. Any slight imperfections, specks of grit or even hairs on hammer face or stake surface can mark the metal. Stakes and hammer faces should be well polished and carefully protected when out of use for this reason.

Planishing should not be carried out until all hard soldering work has been completed. The heat required for this work will anneal the metal and therefore destroy the main effects of planishing.

Because the metal is slightly compressed during planishing it is also slightly expanded. The effect is a little like squeezing a lump of plasticene in the middle. Its outside edges will be pushed outwards. This fact can be used in other situations than finishing beaten work.

Discs of metal, when cut to shape, can often be found not to be flat. Flatness, if needed, can then be a difficult condition to achieve. The wavy surface is caused by one part of the metal being stretched in comparison to another. To partly, or wholly, cure this condition, the non-stretched area should be planished on a flat topped stake to stretch it to match the other areas. If the disc is placed on a flat surface, the stretched area will be that which wants to bend above or below the surface of the other areas.

Square cut plates can also exhibit the same condition and the same methods may be used as a cure. If the raised parts are simply 'bashed' to try to push them down, they will only be stretched more, making the problem worse. Fig. 59 explains the procedure, I hope, better than a lengthy description. The thing is to remember to proceed slowly, using gentle hammer blows with numerous stops to inspect and feel the metal. Feeling the surface gently with the fingers is a good way to detect high spots and hollows.

Forming Curves and Cylinders

Curved work may have much of its shaping, in all but the thickest sheet, carried out with the hands. Watch out for sharp edges though. A good robust former is needed over which to work the metal, a bench mandrel (Fig. 60) being good for this purpose. The size should suit the work, but for general purposes, solid steel 50mm to 75mm (2 to 3 inches) square and around 600mm (2ft) long will be found about right. It is important that the top surface is rounded off.

Alternatively, round steel bar or hard wood held in the vice or fixed to the bench will be found to work well.

For cylinders the development must first be prepared and annealed if necessary. It is then held so that its approximate centre line corresponds with that of the former or mandrel and so that the hands are spread out and flat on the surface, one either side of centre. Press down sufficiently to just curve the metal, then slide it sideways, pressing and bending all the time, until the whole surface has been slightly curved. Then curve the whole surface a little further by the same methods and keep working it in this way until the two edges meet. Beware of pressing too hard, or trying to form too much of the curve in one go. This can result in the cylinder being formed in a series of bends. If this situation does arise, the work may be turned over so that the outside surface rests on the mandrel or former, when more pressure straightens the bend, or a mallet may be used on the bend line from the outside.

When sufficient curving has been done to bring the opposite edges nearly together the shape of the cylinder should be as in Fig. 61(b). The remaining short straight sections should be malleted along their whole length, just beyond the point at which they rest on the mandrel, moved back slightly and hit again, until the edge is reached. Assuming a butt joint, the situation to aim for is when the two edges just meet and the end view of the cylinder shows a true circle. If a seamed joint is to be used, the two halves of the seam need to be formed before curving, and final truing up is carried out after curving the cylinder and closing the seam.

Conical shapes may be formed in a very similar way. A tapered stake or

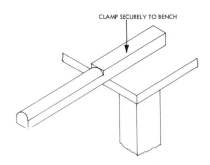

Fig. 60 *Bench mandrel.*

mandrel should be used, and again, it should be of a substantial size, but rather smaller than the final shape required. Funnel stake or bick iron are the most useful when curving conical work by hand. It is less easy, but not impossible, to use a parallel former to bend conical work.

The procedure is the same as for a cylinder, but this time the work must be moved in a curve as it is bent by the pressure of the hands. It is moved so that it follows the approximate course of the radius R, in Fig. 62.

When working with thicker sheet, a mallet may need to be used to provide

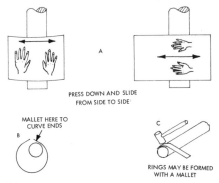

Fig. 61 *Forming curves over a mandrel.*

73

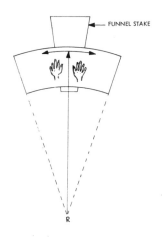

FUNNEL STAKE

R

Fig. 62 *Forming conical work.*

extra pressure as required, but it is surprising how much work it is possible to do with hand pressure alone. In many ways, it is better not to use a mallet on curved work because its effect is very localised. This can lead to uneven curving which may well be diffi-

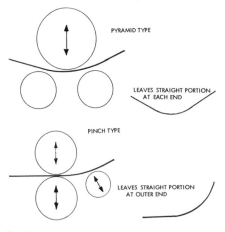

PYRAMID TYPE

LEAVES STRAIGHT PORTION AT EACH END

PINCH TYPE

LEAVES STRAIGHT PORTION AT OUTER END

Fig. 63 *Bending rolls.*

cult to true up. Mallets can also stretch the metal if used carelessly, leading to further shaping problems.

Professionally, curved shapes are usually formed by hand or power operated bending rolls. These have the advantage of producing an accurate curve quickly. They avoid the need for repeated working and checking of the metal whilst forming. Small hand-worked bending rolls are available that are aimed at the model engineer. These are quite suitable for home use and anyone needing to roll thicker sheet to make model boilers, or who is likely to do any large amount of curved work, may well consider a set to be a worthwhile investment.

It may be possible to obtain larger sets of bending rolls second hand from dealers, or as redundant equipment from a local factory. As a general rule, though, most factory equipment of this kind tends to be rather large for home use.

As with most other items of workshop equipment, at least one design suitable for home construction has appeared in *Model Engineer* over the years. The last design for a small set of bending rolls that I recall was by Mr. G. H. Thomas in the 1st October 1976, issue.

There are two types of hand-powered bending rolls, known as pinch or pyramid types. The manner of operation of each kind is shown in Fig. 63. In the pyramid type, the top roller is moved up or down to give greater or lesser radius curves. In the pinch type, the adjustmen of the back roller sets the amount of curvature while the top or bottom driving roller is adjustable to suit the thickness of the metal.

Pyramid rolls tend to leave a flat portion at either end of the work, while the pinch type only leave this at one end. Reversing the work after the first passage through the rolls will remove this with the pinch type. With pyramid rolls, however, the ends have to be curved by some other method. Normal practice is to hammer the straight end over the lower roller as it is fed through, or lever it upwards with a convex curved bar. The former method is used with thinner material and the latter with thicker. For amateur purposes, the pinch type of bending rolls are probably better.

As with hand forming of curved work, it is important to work up to the curve gradually when using rolls and not attempt to form the final shape in one go. It is also better, when rolling cylinders and cones, to over-roll slightly. The natural spring in the metal will cause it to spring outwards as it is removed from rolls. Removal is usually achieved by lifting out the top roller whose bearings are designed to permit this.

Bending rolls are often made with round grooves at one end to permit the bending of wire and rod and work with wired edges.

Circular work is not always cylindrical or conical. Sheets often need to be curved, but not to a full circle. In cases like this, the procedure is the same but bending is stopped as soon as sufficient curvature has been given to the metal. A good example of work of this kind is the cab roof sheet shown in Fig. 64. The sharp curves at either end could be formed by placing over a mandrel or other suitable former and bending with a mallet. Following this, hand pressure or bending rolls would produce the more gently curved central portion.

Flanging

Flanges are needed on sheet metal items for a variety of purposes, but usually to allow one part to be fixed to another. Where the item is of rectangular shape the flange may be made in the same way as the sides of the box already described. It is the way of the craft, however, that the easiest shapes to form seem to be those that are the least frequently required. Most flanging, therefore, seems to need to be carried out in a manner somewhat similar to raising.

A typical situation is where a cylindrical item needs a base or end cap. The blank should be marked out and cut as a disc, the diameter of which is sufficiently over-size to allow the edge to be knocked over to form the flange. The allowance on the diameter for thin material (under 0.5mm – 24 SWG) may simply be twice the flange depth. Above this, twice the metal thickness must be added on as well.

After cutting out and shaping, the blank is annealed, if necessary, and the inside diameter of the flange marked on as a pencil circle. The diameter of this is that of the cylinder it is to fit, less twice the flange depth and the metal thickness. The diagram Fig. 65 will, I hope, make this clear.

Flanges of this type may be formed as shown in Fig. 66(a). The half moon stake is held in the vice and the work held against its vertical edge at a slight

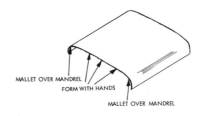

MALLET OVER MANDREL

FORM WITH HANDS

MALLET OVER MANDREL

Fig. 64 Curving a cabroof sheet for a model rail or road locomotive.

75

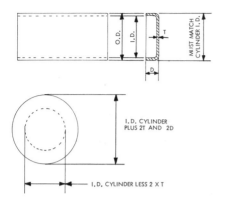

Fig. 65

angle. The pencil circle marking the inside diameter of the flange must exactly coincide with the top edge of the half moon stake and it is then knocked over very slightly with a mallet. Then the metal is turned a little and the next section knocked over slightly, keeping the pencil line at the top of the stake.

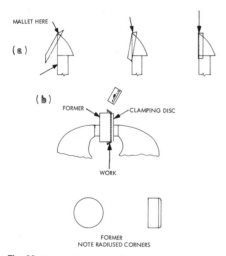

Fig. 66 *Forming a flange on a disc.*

Work all round in this way, then work all round again. Do this repeatedly, re-annealing as soon as the metal feels to be resisting the mallet blows, until the complete flange is formed. As with other work of this sort, if buckles and wrinkles are to be avoided the whole flange must be slightly formed at first and then increased in stages until finished. If any attempt is made to form it all in one go at any single point, buckling will almost certainly occur. This is very difficult to remove once started.

While forming the flange in this way, the flat surface will tend to bow outwards, especially towards the edges. Warping may also occur. Therefore, at intervals during flanging, it is necessary to true up the disc with the mallet on a flat surface, working from the inside. Planishing may also be needed to remove any stretching.

To avoid problems, the method shown in Fig. 66(b) may be used. A former is turned up from hard wood or solid mild steel and a thick clamping disc of similar diameter is made. The blank is prepared as for the previous method and laid on the clamping disc. The former is then laid on the metal and lined up with the pencil circle marking the inside diameter of the flange, so forming a 'sandwich' with the blank between the former and clamping plate. This is then put in the vice and held just tightly enough to stop it falling out. Finger pressure and light mallet blows may be used to make any final adjustments to the position of the three pieces. Then the vice is tightened firmly and the flange partly knocked over for as much of its length as possible. Before turning it in the vice to make the next section accessible to the mallet, the blank, former and clamping disc should be clamped together to keep the align-

ment. Toolmaker's clamps or small G-cramps are quite good for this. Clamp up in the vice again and continue forming in stages until completion.

Sometimes flanged discs of this kind are used as end plates for model 'pot' type steam boilers and other small pressure vessels. It is then best to give some doming, even if only slightly, to the flat surface so that it is less likely to bow under pressure. This feature should be produced by a hollowing process before flanging is carried out. If the blank has a hole in its centre, the clamping disc may be fitted with a pin which passes through the hole in the blank and into a hole in the former and ensures alignment.

The other common situation in which flanging needs to be carried out is on the ends of cylinders. This may be needed to join them to a flat surface, to produce a seam, or to join two cylinders together if making pipe-work or ducting of any kind. They may need to be formed facing outwards or inwards and the method used will depend upon which is required.

Inward facing flanges can be formed by the method shown in Fig. 67. The

drawing should be self-explanatory, the important thing to remember is to work the flange down gradually, as already described for other work of this nature. This is the golden rule of all forming and shaping work. The shape required should be worked up to gradually, in easy stages. Trying to change the shape of the metal too much in one go can only lead to trouble.

Outward facing flanges are best formed with a bossing mallet, working over the edge of a stake, or flat surface, as shown in Fig. 68(a). If several flanges of similar diameter are needed, the device shown in plan view at Fig. 68(b) will assist in holding the work during flang-

ROUND BAR HELD IN VICE

Fig. 67

77

ing. It may be made from thickish steel plate or wood, and the semi-circular cut-outs need to be slightly larger in diameter than the item to be flanged. It may be held in the vice or clamped to the bench, the work held in the cut-out and the flange knocked over as in Fig. 68(a). When working with long tubes, the stake or former should be held so that the tube can be horizontal.

The live steam enthusiasts among model engineers are the people most likely to need flanges on thicker sheet when boiler making. Fortunately, most amateur boiler making is done using copper, which is a soft, easily worked metal. Model boiler making, as in full-size boiler work, requires a lot of fairly advance flanging and it is only possible to give a general guide here. For further information I would recommend any of the specialist books published on the subject.

Fig. 69 shows a typical firebox back plate and the flanging block required to shape it. The block may be of hard wood, steel, or wood faced with steel sheet, depending on what is available. Note the generously rounded corners: it is important to avoid sharp corners in work such as this. The width at any point should be the inside width of the firebox, less twice the thickness of the metal used, and the thickness of the former should be generously more than flange depth.

When cutting out the blanks for this kind of work, remember that the composite curves required can cause the flange to be less deep at the points marked (A) in Fig. 69. The best way of overcoming this is to allow a generous amount of metal for forming the flange and trim to the correct size afterwards. This is a good policy in all work of this kind when the exact size of blank required may not be calculated with much accuracy.

The procedure for knocking the flange over is the same as that for the flat disc described at the start of this section. Again, beware of trying to form too much in one go and re-anneal as soon as the metal loses its 'dead', pliable feel. Any holes required should be drilled and cut after flanging and methods using cold chisels should be avoided in this kind of work since they can cause mis-shaping.

Boxes and Lids

While thinking about forming methods it is appropriate to consider the way to make boxes with fitted lids.

If these need to fit inside or outside the box they need to be made after the main body of the box, be this round, square or rectangular. The blank for the lid may then be marked off from the job and cut out. Its edges may be formed as if they were flanges, using methods appropriate to the shape required. The normal requirement is for a lid to fit

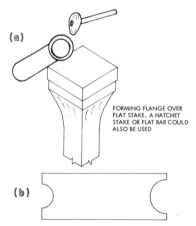

(a)

FORMING FLANGE OVER FLAT STAKE. A HATCHET STAKE OR FLAT BAR COULD ALSO BE USED

(b)

Fig. 68

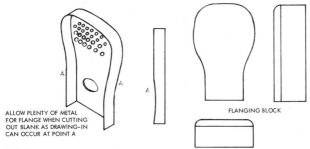

ALLOW PLENTY OF METAL
FOR FLANGE WHEN CUTTING
OUT BLANK AS DRAWING-IN
CAN OCCUR AT POINT A

FLANGING BLOCK

Fig. 69 *Firebox backplate for model boiler.*

around the outside of such a box, but if it has to fit inside a lip must be fixed around the inside to stop it falling right in. This can be made from a flat strip soldered in place.

When lids have to be an exact fit, their sides being flush with those of the box, it is best to make the lid and the box in one piece and then saw off the lid. A development is cut out as if making an open topped box. This is then folded

and bent to shape but the bottom will become the lid. A separate bottom is made and fitted, following which the top section is sawn off to make the lid. Fig. 70 illustrates the procedure which is the best way, using hand tools, to ensure a lid of identical shape and size to the box. The method may be used for both round or rectangular boxes and will find most use in work whose appearance is important.

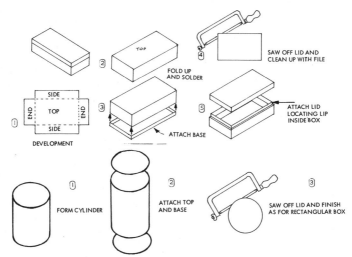

Fig. 70 *Making boxes with flush-fitting lids.*

79

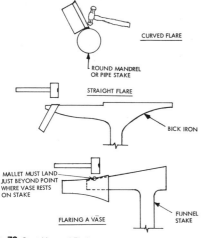

Fig. 71 *Contracting the end of a cylinder.*

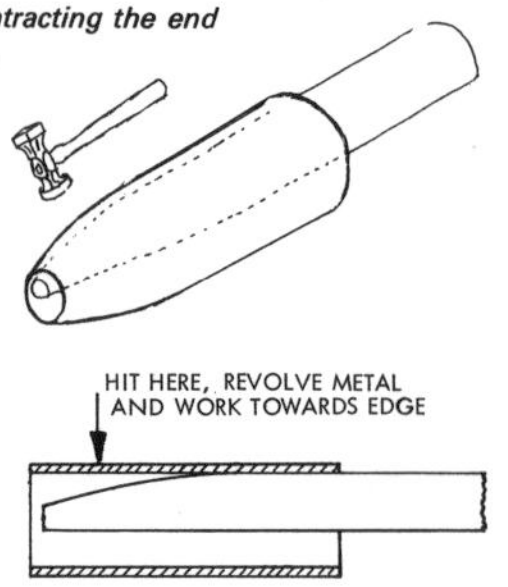

HIT HERE, REVOLVE METAL AND WORK TOWARDS EDGE

Stretching and Flaring

Cylindrical components and rings for bases, whether made by raising or by rolling, can need to be flared. The methods shown in Fig. 72 may be used, again with hammers or mallets as required. As said before, work up to the shape gradually.

Contracting

The ends of cylindrical work may be contracted, if necessary, by the method shown in Fig. 71. The stake must be made to a size and profile to suit the work, which is then placed over it and shaped, using a planishing hammer or mallet.

REVOLVE THE RING UNDER THE HAMMER

Fig. 73 *Expanding a ring.*

CURVED FLARE

ROUND MANDREL OR PIPE STAKE

STRAIGHT FLARE

BICK IRON

MALLET MUST LAND JUST BEYOND POINT WHERE VASE RESTS ON STAKE

FUNNEL STAKE

FLARING A VASE

Fig. 72 *Stretching and Flaring.*

Expanding Rings

When making rings to fit inside cylindrical work, they can often be found to be a little too loose. So long as the error is small, the ring may be expanded by placing over a round mandrel held in the vice and planishing on the outside. The slight reduction in wall thickness which this causes stretches the ring and increases its diameter. It must be stressed that this increase is only slight and the range over which it is effective is rather limited (Fig. 73).

This method is useful when a tight-fitting ring is needed. It may be deliberately made slightly under size and expanded by planishing, until it is a suitably tight fit.

CHAPTER 5

Seams, Edge Finishes, Joints

Seams are used principally, but not exclusively, in tinplate work for joining edges. They are also used for joining ends, bases etc. to containers. Metals other than tinplate may be joined by the use of seams if they are sufficiently thin, but this is not as commonplace.

Apart from those already described, three special tools are required for seaming work, although, as in many things, improvisation is possible. These are a peining or tucking hammer, a creasing iron and a seam set, or groover. Fig. 74 illustrates them.

The normal range of seams in use is shown in Fig. 75, along with their names. It is worth remembering that the names used to describe any given seam may vary. For example, that described here as a folded seam also may be called a grooved seam or a hook seam, depending which book you read. For many, the production methods are obvious from the drawings but others will be described.

The easiest way to join the edges of two pieces of sheet metal is to place one on top of the other so that they overlap slightly. Rivets or solder may be used to hold them together. This is the lap joint, quite useful with thicker

metal, or where a quick job is required. Its strength however, comes from the solder or rivets and when working with thin material it does not do much to provide any extra stiffness. It also cannot give a flush surface to both sides of the work. However, it is of use in many situations.

When a flush surface is needed, the butt joint is used. The edges are simply butted together and soldered, brazed or

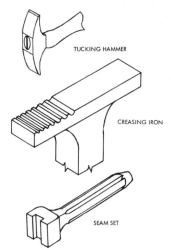

Fig. 74

81

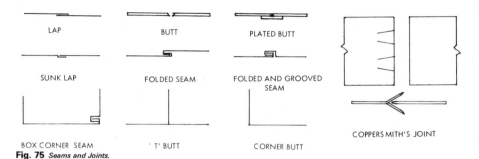

LAP

BUTT

PLATED BUTT

SUNK LAP

FOLDED SEAM

FOLDED AND GROOVED SEAM

COPPERSMITH'S JOINT

BOX CORNER SEAM

'T' BUTT

CORNER BUTT

Fig. 75 *Seams and Joints.*

welded, depending on the metal used and its thickness. This is not of much use with tinplate because the strength of the soft solder is insufficient to withstand normal use, and higher temperature solders cannot be used.

The butt joint finds most use with copper or brass work when hard solder is used. It can, if carefully made, give an invisible joint. Thicker steel sheet is also frequently butt jointed and welded to

produce many familiar structures such as ships' hulls and motor car body sections. Butt joints in aluminium are also possible with some of the modern aluminium solders.

When greater strength is needed, when only one side of the work needs a flush surface, or when rivets are used to fasten the joint, the plated butt joint is used. Its greatest use is on riveted work.

The sunk lap joint is used when one side of the work needs to be flat but a lap joint is sufficient. It relies on the joining method for its strength and may be soft or hard soldered or spot welded, depending on the metal used and the item.

Special crimping pliers are available for making the sunken part, but it may be produced by other methods. Fig. 76 shows one way to do this. Two stout steel bars are cut a little longer than the seam required. Narrow strips of scrap metal, the same thickness as that used for the work, are soldered on to these to form a step. Note the double thickness on the female half. The work can then be pressed between these in a vice as in Fig. 76(a). Nuts and bolts may be used to exert the pressure instead, as in Fig. 76(b).

Fig. 76(c) shows a third method, where only one stepped block needs to be made. The work is clamped to this

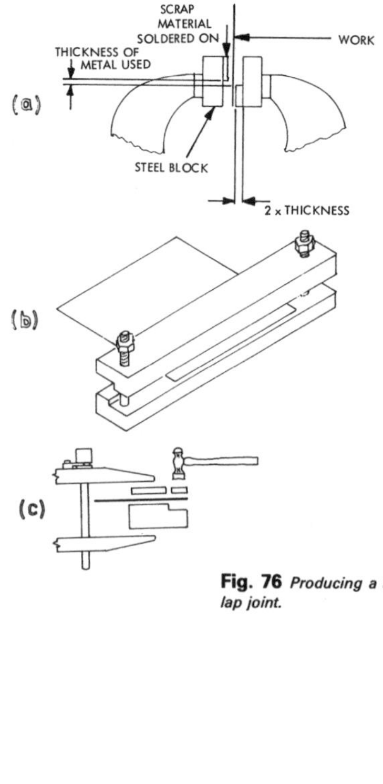

SCRAP MATERIAL SOLDERED ON

WORK

THICKNESS OF METAL USED

(a)

STEEL BLOCK

2 x THICKNESS

(b)

(c)

Fig. 76 *Producing a sunk lap joint.*

and shaping is carried out using a hammer and steel block.

The folded seam (Fig. 75) may be soldered, but will hold itself together without this. Because the seam consists of four thicknesses of metal it is quite effective in stiffening the finished work. If soldered it is, also, unlikely to leak. To make this seam, a strip, cut out from scrap material, the same thickness as the job, is needed. This is called a gauging strip. Both edges have a narrow

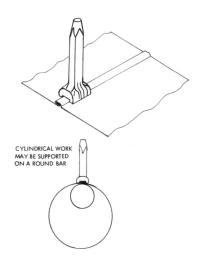

CYLINDRICAL WORK MAY BE SUPPORTED ON A ROUND BAR

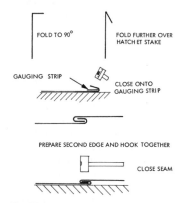

FOLD TO 90°

FOLD FURTHER OVER HATCHET STAKE

GAUGING STRIP

CLOSE ONTO GAUGING STRIP

PREPARE SECOND EDGE AND HOOK TOGETHER

CLOSE SEAM

Fig. 77 *Making a folded seam.*

Fig. 78 *Setting down a folded and grooved seam.*

strip (5mm (³⁄₁₆″) is a common allowance) folded to 90° then folded further over the hatchet stake. The gauging strip is placed inside the angle of one, and it is knocked down onto the strip. After this has been repeated with the second edge, the two edges are pulled together, rested on a flat surface and closed with a mallet. Fig. 77 shows these stages and may be easier to understand than a written description. If care is taken, it is a reasonably easy seam to make.

The folded seam has the disadvantage that both sides of the work end up with a ridge or step. Where one side

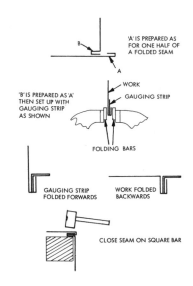

'A' IS PREPARED AS FOR ONE HALF OF A FOLDED SEAM

'B' IS PREPARED AS 'A' THEN SET UP WITH GAUGING STRIP AS SHOWN

WORK

GAUGING STRIP

FOLDING BARS

GAUGING STRIP FOLDED FORWARDS

WORK FOLDED BACKWARDS

CLOSE SEAM ON SQUARE BAR

Fig. 79 *Making a box seam.*

must have a flat surface, the folded and grooved seam is used. This is produced in the same way as the folded seam, but after closing, it is set down using a seam set (Fig. 78). Folded and grooved seams can be found on most food tins.

A box seam is used when a stronger corner joint than that given by simply bending over and soldering a tab is required. It also leaves both the outside faces flush. Fig. 79 shows the way this seam is made. Both sides are first prepared as for the folded seam. The one that is bent outwards is then held in folding bars with a gauge strip inserted. The gauge strip is folded forwards and the box side backwards, then removed from the folding bars. A vice or pliers may be used to grip the gauge strip so that it may be pulled out, then the seam is assembled and closed with a mallet.

The coppersmith's joint is used to join two straight edges when a really strong job is required. It is little used in decorative work but is quite useful in the production of copper boilers if the barrel is being rolled from sheet. The fingers of the joint are produced by shearing along the dovetail lines. They are then bent alternately up and down and thinned by filing towards their outer edge. Before closing the joint, the mating surfaces must be cleaned and fluxed so that they can be soldered afterwards. Because of the comparatively large surface area to take the solder, this is a strong joint.

The 'T' and corner butt joints are simply produced by soldering. They rely entirely on the strength of the solder and are only used for light duty work. Such joints are widely used in making small scale models from thin sheet, for example. An exception to this is when working in steel sheet when such joints could be strongly made by welding. Together with the butt joint, they are about the only ones used in straightforward welded assemblies.

Fig. 80 depicts the various standard bottom joints and seams used for fixing bottoms or ends onto cylindrical containers, although there is really no reason why they cannot be adapted for use on rectangular work. Again, work in the thicker sizes of steel sheet is normally butt jointed and welded.

The snuffed seam consists of a circular disc with a flange knocked up around its edge which is then used to solder it to the sides of the container. Its derivatives, the flat inset and anti-wear inset are made in the same way, with due allowance on diameter to fit inside the work. No matter how carefully marked out and made, it is extremely difficult to produce hand

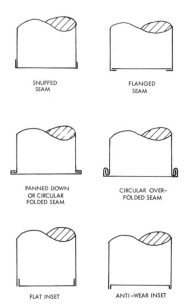

SNUFFED SEAM

FLANGED SEAM

PANNED DOWN OR CIRCULAR FOLDED SEAM

CIRCULAR OVER-FOLDED SEAM

FLAT INSET

ANTI-WEAR INSET

Fig. 80 *Circular seams and joints.*

formed flanges to within the exact limits required for a good fit. A better, more reliable method is to make the end or base before soldering the sides together. These can then be curved and pushed into or held around the base and soldered to it. The joint along the sides may be soldered afterwards. Wire may be tightened around the sides to hold them together while soldering on the base.

This method could also be used with a folded seam joining the sides. First shape and bend the cylinder. Along one of the joining edges form half the seam. Cut out and flange the base, hold the sides in place around the base and mark off where the second half of the seam needs to come. Form this second half, then assemble the sides in or around the base as before, and close the seam. Finally solder everything up. Remember that the side seam must finish short of the end by a sufficient amount to permit the base to fit on (Fig. 81).

Snuffed-on bottoms are suitable for much work, but are dependent on the strength of the solder used. For general containers they are quite satisfactory, and are frequently used to fix the ends on to 'pot' boilers for small low pressure steam driven models. The anti-wear inset does, indeed, reduce wear on the base. It also means that a container so fitted will stand without wobbling, even if the base becomes slightly domed.

The flanged seam is used when strength is required that does not depend just upon the solder. Little need be said about its production. A flange is knocked over, inwards, on the end of the container. The base disc is then cut and filed to fit and soldered in position.

The panned down seam is used when a stronger joint is needed, or one that is

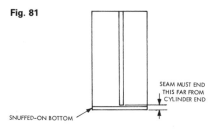

Fig. 81

SEAM MUST END THIS FAR FROM CYLINDER END

SNUFFED-ON BOTTOM

more easily made liquid-tight. To make it, the bottom edge of the cylinder is flanged outwards and the base disc is flanged. Both are assembled and the flange on the base disc is knocked over that on the cylinder, as shown in Fig. 82. It is finally closed tight using the tucking hammer. Be careful to avoid touching the sides with mallet or hammer.

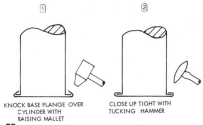

KNOCK BASE FLANGE OVER CYLINDER WITH RAISING MALLET

CLOSE UP TIGHT WITH TUCKING HAMMER

Fig. 82

Because it projects outwards the panned down seam is often inconvenient. When this is the case, it may be made into an over-folded seam. After completion, the panned down seam is

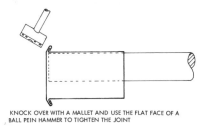

KNOCK OVER WITH A MALLET AND USE THE FLAT FACE OF A BALL PEIN HAMMER TO TIGHTEN THE JOINT

Fig. 83

85

folded flat against the sides of the work on a bar or mandrel as in Fig. 83. The only other difference is that the inner edge of the panned down bottom should, if it is to be made into an over-folded seam, be at least the metal thickness away from the sides of the container. If this clearance is not allowed it will be very hard to fold it up without distortion.

Edge Finishes
Edge finishes are necessary on exposed edges when making items from thin sheet, partly for reasons of safety. A 'raw' edge forms a very close approximation to a razor! The other reason for using them is to help stiffen the work.

They are most frequently used when working in tinplate, but may be used with any metal. Brass and copper work and items made from thicker sheet are often edged with half round beading which is available in various widths, and may be bolted, riveted or soldered in place. Angle section can also be used for this purpose. Cut-outs in locomotive cab side-sheets are often edged with half-round beading.

Sufficient extra material to produce an edge finish, if required, must be allowed when marking out developments.

The normal methods used for finishing edges are shown in Fig. 84. Of them all, the safe edge, or false bead as it is sometimes known, is the quickest and easiest to form. First, the width required

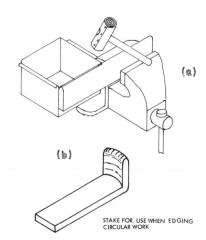

(a)

(b)

STAKE FOR, USE WHEN EDGING CIRCULAR WORK

Fig. 85 *Forming an open folded edge.*

(usually around 5mm (³⁄₁₆)) is folded to a right angle in folding bars and then beyond a right angle over a hatchet stake. Finally, the work is placed on a flat surface (the bench will do, but the bench block is better) and a mallet is used to knock the folded edge flat onto the metal. Solder may or may not be used to finish it off, as desired, but is advisable on tinplate items that are likely to get wet. In this way, the bare steel of the cut edge is protected.

The double hem is made by making a safe edge as above and then repeating the process to fold it back over itself again. Sufficient material must be allowed on the development to form the second fold. This should be the same amount again as for the first fold, plus an amount equal to the thickness of the metal used.

In my experience, the open fold edge is not often used. It would be formed by knocking it over a curved edge former held in the vice, as shown in Fig. 85.

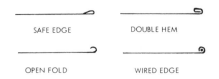

SAFE EDGE   DOUBLE HEM

OPEN FOLD   WIRED EDGE

Fig. 84 *Edge finishes.*

86

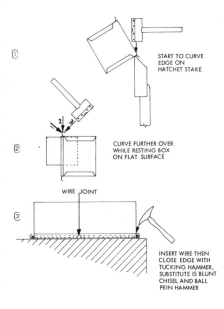

(1) START TO CURVE EDGE ON HATCHET STAKE

(2) CURVE FURTHER OVER WHILE RESTING BOX ON FLAT SURFACE

WIRE JOINT

(3) INSERT WIRE THEN CLOSE EDGE WITH TUCKING HAMMER. SUBSTITUTE IS BLUNT CHISEL AND BALL PEIN HAMMER

Fig. 86 *Wiring an edge.*

Wired edges give a very strong job and are found in many situations. The old oil-lit railway hand lamps, metal pouring funnels and watering cans are common items on which to find wired edges. As the name suggests, the edge of the metal is rolled around a piece of wire. The wire, being thicker than the metal used, and the effect of the rolling, provide a considerable stiffening effect.

The production of wired edges requires care if a neat job is to be produced. The exact method used will depend upon the shape of the item being edged. All wiring should start, however, by marking off the amount needed to form the edge. This should be equal to 2½ x the diameter of the wire to be used. The size of wire is not too critical and often depends upon what is to hand. It should 'look right' when seen against the item for which it is intended. Remember that the finished edge will be considerably larger in diameter, when finished, than the wire around which it is rolled.

Square or rectangular work should, if possible, have wired edges started before any other shaping is done. Then they may be formed in folding bars with one rounded corner and brought to the same stage as the open folded edge. After shaping the item, wiring may be completed.

Where the work is such that shaping has to take place first, then the easiest way to form the wired edges is over the hatchet stake. This is the method illustrated in Fig. 86. Start with just the smallest amount of metal peeping over the top of the hatchet stake and gently tap all the way along it with a mallet. The aim is to slightly bend it, not produce a sharp fold. Move the metal up a

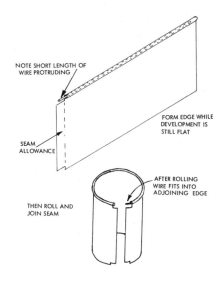

NOTE SHORT LENGTH OF WIRE PROTRUDING

FORM EDGE WHILE DEVELOPMENT IS STILL FLAT

SEAM ALLOWANCE

AFTER ROLLING WIRE FITS INTO ADJOINING EDGE

THEN ROLL AND JOIN SEAM

Fig. 87 *Wired edge on circular work.*

little and repeat the procedure with the mallet. Keep moving the metal up a little at a time and using the mallet, until the correct shape has been produced. This should appear, at this stage, to be the same as the open folded edge.

Circular work requiring wired edges should also, when possible, have these formed before the item is bent to shape, while it is still flat. Similar methods to those used for rectangular work may then be employed. The wired edge is completed, leaving a short end of wire sticking out which slides into the wired edge at the opposite end, after rolling (see Fig. 87).

If circular work has to have the edges formed after bending to shape, proceed as for forming a flange. The flange may then be worked to the correct 'U' shape over a similar stake to that in Fig. 86.

Whichever procedure is used, the wired edge should first be brought to a 'U' shape like the over-folded edge. The wire may then be bent to shape and dropped into place, taking care to see that the join in the wire does not coincide with any seams or joints in the work. With a rectangular item, the wire joint should be in the middle of one side. With circular work, if wiring after bending, make the joint come opposite, or nearly opposite, the seam. If wiring before bending this is not really possible, but it may still be made to come a little way away from the seam, as shown in Fig. 87.

Once the wire is in place the edge needs to be completely rolled around it and 'tucked in' behind it. This rolling process is started with the edge of a mallet while resting the metal on a flat surface, as in Fig. 86. It is finished by using the tucking hammer, again as in Fig. 86. Tucking hammers have fairly sharp edges, so they should be care-

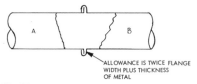

Fig. 88

fully used to make sure they land exactly where required. Otherwise, the sides of the work will become bruised and scarred, a sign of careless or unskilled work.

Flanged Pipe Joint

Fig. 88 shows the way in which sections of piping may be joined. The joint could be used with solid drawn tubing or with pipework made by rolling from sheet. Obviously, it is only applicable to thin walled piping or tube.

To produce this joint, part (A) on Fig. 88 is flanged. Part (B) is then given a larger flange, sufficient to allow it to be formed over the one on part (A).

The flange on part (B) then needs to be flanged again over the half moon stake, or the end of a suitable round former, held in the vice. This is shown in Fig. 89.

Finally, the two pieces are placed together and the flange on part (B) is knocked over that on part (A). It is closed tight using a tucking hammer. Fig. 90 shows the stages in forming the joint.

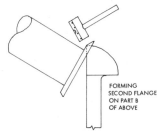

Fig. 89

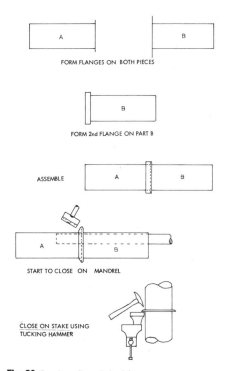

FORM FLANGES ON BOTH PIECES

FORM 2nd FLANGE ON PART B

ASSEMBLE

START TO CLOSE ON MANDREL

CLOSE ON STAKE USING
TUCKING HAMMER

Fig. 90 *Forming a flanged pipe joint.*

Flanged pipe joints may also be used at angles other than 90° to the centre line of the pipe to produce joints on corners. Similar methods may be used for forming them but due allowance must be made on the development for the flange. The development for the pipe elbow that appears in Chapter 3 is the one that would be used in this situation.

Caulking

This term is sometimes used to describe a hammering process used for thickening the edges of raised work, but here it is used in the sense of making vessels liquid-tight.

When items are assembled by soldering, welding or brazing, so long as the work is properly carried out there is no problem. Filling with water is the most convenient way to check for leaks. Any slight ones can usually be cured by further soldering.

It is when rivets or threaded fittings are used for the assembly work that problems can occur. The traditional way of making larger riveted structures tight is to work round the edges of the rivet heads and plates with a caulking chisel in the manner shown in Fig. 91. This is not a very suitable method for the size of work that the amateur home mechanic is likely to produce, however. His needs can be better served by other methods.

Articles like model boilers, water and fuel tanks, if using rivets as the main means of fastening the sections together, can often most conveniently be caulked using soft solder. More will be said about soldering methods later on but it is important to remember in this sort of work that a soldering iron alone will not, in most cases, give sufficient heat. For all except small work extra heat, such as from a blowlamp, will be required. It is important to make sure that the work is cleaned before riveting. Flux, of the liquid type, can be run into

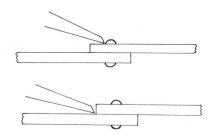

Fig. 91 *Caulking rivet heads and plate edges with a caulking chisel.*

the joints afterwards. Then the work is heated generally, with the blowlamp or torch and the iron used to apply the solder, which should be encouraged to run well into all the joints and around the rivet heads. This method is quite successful with copper, brass or mild steel structures, or, indeed, any metal that will take soft solder well. Fortunately, most work of this sort uses these metals. It is also important that the temperatures to which such work is subjected in use do not exceed the melting point of soft solder.

For higher temperatures, or metals which are difficult to solder, other methods must be used. First, it must be said that wherever possible materials and methods should be chosen which avoid these problems. Where higher temperatures need to be withstood, it is better to hard solder or braze the work together, rather than use rivets and soft solder caulking. When using rivets it is best to avoid choosing metals which are difficult to solder. However, it is not always possible to choose the ideal situation, especially in repair work.

For caulking work only subject to low temperatures, resin filler paste is probably as good as anything. An alternative is to use a mastic gun of the type used for sealing around windows and wash basins. The standard size gun is rather cumbersome for some of the smaller modelling work. The smaller type, sold for sealing joints between tiles and baths may be more useful here. These items are readily obtainable from builders' merchants and ironmongers.

When higher temperatures need to be withstood, one of the commercial gasket jointings or jointing paste for car exhaust systems can be worked into the joints and around the rivets. If using exhaust jointing paste, remember that it

is, basically, a ceramic material, and is cured by heating, not ageing or chemical action. It should be gently heated for some time until hard before expecting it to withstand water. Otherwise it will be washed away when the vessel is filled.

Where threaded fittings are used to fix components together (e.g. studs and nuts around a flange), a gasket is probably the best means of sealing the joint. These can be made from cartridge or brown paper, cork or proper sheet gasket material. They can be marked off the job and cut out with scissors using small punches for any holes required. Do not try to use a drill. Paper gaskets can be made by using a hammer, a surprisingly effective method. The ball pein may be used to cut around the inside of round holes (see Fig. 92).

Before assembling, gaskets should be smeared with a good jointing paste, as should all screw threads. There are many jointing pastes available in motor car accessory shops but 'Hermetite' is a very well known one. Plumbers' pipe jointing paste may also be used and various types of this may be obtained at builders' merchants.

Plastic gasket-making pastes are available, also from car accessory shops. These do away with the need for separate gaskets.

Jointing pastes should be used fairly generously, especially around screw threads. They are not gap fillers, however, and the mating surfaces should always be as clean and smooth and as good a fit as possible.

After assembly, all work of the kind under consideration here needs testing for leaks. For anything of a tank-like nature that simply has to hold a liquid the time-honoured method is to fill it with water. It is then left to stand for a while, being inspected at intervals, until all leaks are marked or until it is decided that there are no leaks. In my own experience, it is unusual to find no leaks in the first test!

Commercial leak detectors are available but are rather expensive. The type I have used consists of two parts, each in an aerosol can. One is a white powdery substance and is sprayed on one side of the work. The other is a red penetrant liquid with very low surface tension that is sprayed on to the opposite side of the work. Any leaks show up as red spots that are clearly visible against the white spray, which is very absorbent.

If a material with lower surface tension than water is required meths is a possibility, but be alert to the fire risk. Also a little washing-up liquid in water will help to reduce its surface tension and could help in detecting small leaks.

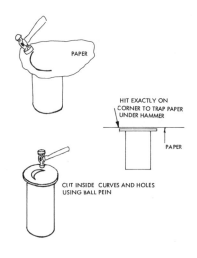

PAPER

HIT EXACTLY ON CORNER TO TRAP PAPER UNDER HAMMER

PAPER

CUT INSIDE CURVES AND HOLES USING BALL PEIN

Fig. 92 *Cutting out paper gaskets with a ball pein hammer.*

CHAPTER 6

Soldering, Hard Soldering and Brazing

Soldering is the name given to processes where metals are joined together by melting another metal, the solder, around the joint. Obviously, the solder must have a lower melting point than the metals it is being used to join. It adheres to these metals by becoming absorbed by their surface layers.

There are several different forms of soldering, but before considering these individually, a few general comments on the process are in order.

The big enemies of good soldered joints are oil, grease, oxide and any kind of dirt. Therefore, an early stage in any soldering work is to clean the area around the required joint. Rust and oxide can be removed by files and emery cloth. Oxides from heating copper and brass may often be removed by pickling. Grease and oil may be wiped off, or, in more serious cases, treated with detergent or a commercial de-greasant.

Next to dirt, the most common cause of failure in soldering seems to be insufficient heat. It is important to ensure that any heating system used will bring the work to a temperature suitable to melt the solder. Also, and this is something which is often not appreciated,

there needs to be a sufficient volume of heat to cope with the size of the work. For metalworking use, it is usually better for heating equipment to be larger than needed, rather than the other way round.

All forms of soldering require a flux. There are many different kinds, and it is important to use a type suitable for the solder in use and the metals being soldered. Generally it may be said that fluxes prevent the formation of oxide that would otherwise occur during heating and assist the solder to flow. Some have a cleaning action in addition to this function. Excessive use of flux should be avoided since it can create cleaning problems, but do not be mean with it, either.

Whilst it is occasionally possible to use them as such, solders are not fillers. Joints should, therefore, be as close-fitting as possible, with no large gaps.

Solders are made with many different melting points and it is worth having a selection available to use. When a number of joints in close proximity need to be soldered, and they cannot all be done at the same time, the first uses the highest melting point of solder. The others then follow, each using a lower melting point solder, so avoiding the melting of earlier work.

Soldering is considered to have two branches and these are called soft and hard. Soft soldering uses the lower temperatures and is usually carried out with a soldering iron. Hard soldering needs rather more sophisticated heating equipment to attain the higher temperatures required.

TOOLS AND EQUIPMENT

Soldering Irons

For soft soldering, the soldering iron is the most important piece of equipment. There are many types from which to choose and some thought should be given to the kind of work to be attempted when deciding which ones to obtain. Probably more than one will be needed.

Some comment has already been made about soldering irons in the chapter on tools. At the risk of being repetitive it has been my experience that, for the sort of work under consideration here, the traditional, externally heated type of iron is the best choice. When using these, it is common practice, but not essential, to work with two irons. One is heated while one is in use. During a long job, they are exchanged at intervals as the one in use becomes cooled.

Apart from the heating method used, there are, basically, two types of soldering irons. Externally heated versions of these are shown in Fig. 93. The straight-bit iron is used for general purpose work, while the hatchet bit one is used for seams. Its shape helps to spread the heat along the line of the seam. The adjustable type will do both sorts of work.

The size of electric soldering irons is measured by their wattage. Externally heated irons are measured by their weight, 8oz being a common size for general work. The bigger the work, the bigger the iron required. If suitable sized copper bar can be obtained in small quantities it is quite easy to make externally heated soldering irons.

Other Heating Equipment

A blowlamp of some kind is fairly essential, especially for hard soldering work. It is also useful for heating soldering irons. Much work can be done with the paraffin type blowlamp and it is certainly cheap to run when a long job is involved. Temperature-wise, however, it is inferior to the modern ones working off butane or propane gas. Several different makes are available and are quite widely advertised in the various hobby magazines. For hard soldering for boiler making work, a propane torch is probably the best choice for the average home user.

Gas and compressed air blow torches are very good for hard soldering work, but normally require a mains gas supply in the workshop and a com-

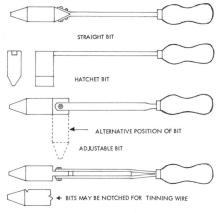

STRAIGHT BIT

HATCHET BIT

ALTERNATIVE POSITION OF BIT

ADJUSTABLE BIT

◄ BITS MAY BE NOTCHED FOR TINNING WIRE

Fig. 93 *Soldering irons.*

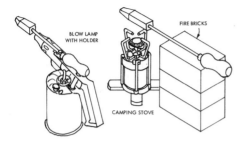

BLOW LAMP
WITH HOLDER

FIRE BRICKS

CAMPING STOVE

Fig. 94 *Heating soldering irons.*

pressor. Most home workers will not, therefore, consider one of these, although in many ways they are the ideal tool.

Oxy-acetylene equipment, again, is not the sort of thing to which most amateurs working at home will give high priority. However, if available, it does make brazing work very much easier.

Holding Tools
One problem in soldering is that of holding the work, either to hold it together until soldered or to move it around during soldering.

Tongs of various kinds will be found useful in most soldering work. For soft soldering, wooden spring-type clothes pegs are very useful holding and clamping devices. They do not conduct away heat from the join being made and remain cool to handle.

For holding work together for hard soldering, soft iron wire is often bound around the work and removed afterwards. G-cramps may be of occasional use in larger work.

Using pliers, as tongs, unless they are old or cheap ones obtained especially for the purpose, should be avoided. The better types of pliers have hardened grips which will become softened if

allowed to get hot. They can also be harmed by corrosive fluxes.

A very useful type of tongs for handling small soldering work are the scissors-like ones used in handling test tubes and such in chemistry work. These are often seen on sale at model engineering exhibitions. Of course plastic, or plastic coated, tongs should not be used with hard soldered work.

Other Equipment
Small paintbrushes are often recommended for applying fluxes to the work but I have never found them very successful. Many fluxes are corrosive and fairly soon eat away the metal sheathing around the bristles, causing them to fall out. I find it better to use a short piece of wooden dowel for applying liquid fluxes, or dead matches may also be used. For hard soldering fluxes, which are often in powder form and are mixed with water before use, broken hacksaw blades make good spatulas.

For containers and mixing pots for fluxes in use, small glass or plastic dishes are good. Old fishpaste jars and pots seem to be just the right size. Only enough flux for the work in hand should be tipped out or mixed up, the rest staying in the supplier's container.

Odd sticks and small pieces of wood in assorted sizes, some with pointed ends, will be found useful for holding and manipulating soft soldered work. They can be used in all sorts of ways, but one example is when one piece needs to be held down on another for soldering. The ideal place to hold it is near where the joint will be, but holding here will mean burnt fingers. A strip of wood laid along the joint will permit the fingers to press the work together without being burnt.

Hard soldering work should always

FIG. 95 – TABLE OF SOFT SOLDERS

Solder Type	Lead	Tin	Others	Melting Point/ Range	Uses
Plumber's	66%	34%	—	183°C to 240°C	Wiped joints on lead
Tinman's	50%	50%	—	185°C to 204°C	General purpose work
Tinman's Fine	34.4%	65%	0.6% Antimony	183°C to 185°C	Electrical work and other places where quick solidification is necessary
Pewterer's	25%	25%	50% Bismuth	96°C to 112°C	Joints in pewter and white metal

take place on a fireproof surface, since a torch or blowlamp of some kind is necessary. A steel bench or hearth surfaced with fire bricks forms a good base on which to work. A biscuit tin containing broken pieces of firebrick makes a good hearth for small work and if only a wooden bench is available a steel sheet or tray can be laid over it for protection. Pieces of firebricks are also needed to place around the work to reflect stray heat from the torch back to where it is needed.

Fire bricks, in various sizes, are obtainable from builders' merchants in small or large quantities. Thin ones also make a good surface on which to carry out soft soldering work, although this may take place on a wood surface because of the lower temperatures involved.

A supply of reasonably clean water will be found useful for washing off pickled work and liquid fluxes. My own workshop water supply is provided by a water butt fed from the roof. This is normally adequate for the purpose mentioned above. Running water would be nice, but a luxury.

Soft Soldering (General Comments)
This process uses solders which are alloys of lead and tin. The proportions are varied and, occasionally, other metals added to give different grades and types of solder. Fig. 95 gives details of what are generally considered to be the grades in which soft solders are available. Now a word of warning. The details of solders given here are those which are generally considered to be 'typical' and are not taken from any one manufacturer's specifications. Experience has shown that there can be variations between the products of different firms. I have, therefore, always found it better to think in terms of broad types of solder rather than particular makes. Most firms will usually supply technical details of their products, if asked, and it is then possible to see into which broad group a particular solder will fit.

The type of solder that will be of most use in general sheet metalwork is that known as 'tinman's', which usually consists of equal parts of tin and lead. Tinman's fine solder is often supplied as wire with flux contained in its centre. It is of most use in small work.

Fluxes are usually selected to suit the metal being soldered and the type of work. For soft soldering, they may be considered as either active or passive. Active fluxes are those which are corrosive and must, therefore, be washed off after soldering, but which, also, have some cleaning effect on the work. Passive fluxes are those which are non-corrosive. They have, usually, no cleaning action but do not need to be washed off afterwards. Passive fluxes can, however, prevent paint adhering to metal surfaces, and in this case they may also need removing after soldering has taken place.

The standard fluxes for use in soft soldering work are listed in Fig. 96, together with the sort of work for which they are intended. Zinc chloride, commonly available as 'Baker's soldering fluid', is the most useful flux for the general purpose soft soldering of sheet metal items. Resin fluxes, whilst useful in electrical work because they do not need to be washed off, are not so good for the kind of work described here. They can be used, however, and are often advised, if using electric soldering irons. 'Yorkshire Flux' and 'Fluxite' are two well known trade names for resin fluxes. If using them the cleaning of work before soldering must be more thorough than when using the active types.

A resin type flux that has come on the market during the last few years is that known as 'Laco Flux', made by the Lake Chemical Co. of Chicago. While being non-acidic, this does seem, as claimed on the jar, to have some cleaning action. It needs to be wiped off after soldering, but is a useful alternative to the traditional resin fluxes when it is difficult to clean the work perfectly. It is stocked by suppliers of building and plumbing materials for use in soldering the copper pipes of central heating systems, but will work with most other common metals.

Dilute hydrochloric acid is shown as being suitable for soldering zinc and galvanised steel because it is usually quoted as the flux for this work. My own experience suggests, however, that galvanised steel may be readily soft soldered using the ordinary zinc chloride flux.

From time to time one hears of other materials being useful as soft soldering fluxes. One which is often recommended is the rust remover 'Jenolite'. I have no personal experience of its use but many people appear to think highly of it, especially for use with the low melting point pewterer's solder in the assembly of white-metal model kits.

It is worth acquiring a variety of fluxes to suit the types of work to be attempted.

Before leaving the subject of fluxes, remember that many, especially the liquid ones, give off fumes when heated. Avoid inhaling these as they can be harmful and are unpleasant. Always work in a reasonably well venti-

FIG. 96 – TABLE OF SOFT SOLDERING FLUXES

Name	Type	Uses
Zinc Chloride	Active	General soldering of brass, copper, steel, tinplate and nickel-silver
Resin/Paste	Passive	Electrical work and any other situation where flux cannot be washed off easily. General work
Dilute Hydrochloric Acid	Active	Zinc and galvanised steel
Tallow	Passive	Lead
Gallipoli Oil	Passive	Pewter and white metal

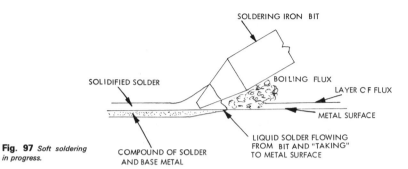

SOLDERING IRON BIT

SOLIDIFIED SOLDER

BOILING FLUX

LAYER C F FLUX

METAL SURFACE

LIQUID SOLDER FLOWING
FROM BIT AND "TAKING"
TO METAL SURFACE

COMPOUND OF SOLDER
AND BASE METAL

Fig. 97 *Soft soldering in progress.*

lated place. If possible, though, avoid soldering out of doors or in a draught as this will make heating the work more difficult.

Procedure
The process of soft soldering is illustrated diagrammatically in Fig. 97. Starting with a new soldering iron, it is first necessary to tin the bit. This means coating it with a thin layer of solder, and is necessary to allow the bit to easily pick up solder during working. First heat the iron to a temperature a little above the melting point of the solder. With electric irons this is taken care of automatically, and is simply a matter of leaving them switched on until well warmed up. For externally heated irons, wait until a short time after the heating flame turns a bright green colour.

Next clean the bit. This can be done by dipping it in flux or rubbing with a wire brush or old file or a combination of these procedures. Dip a stick of solder in flux and immediately the bit is cleaned, rub the solder over its end. Wipe off any surplus solder with a damp cloth and the soldering iron is now ready for use. It may be returned to the heating stove until needed, but, with an externally heated soldering iron, do not leave it there long enough

for it to become over-heated. This will boil away the solder and burn the bit which will then require cleaning and tinning all over again. Soldering iron bits become corroded and pitted with use and require periodic filing to re-shape them.

Work for soldering should first be cleaned then both parts of the joint coated with flux. Excessive use of flux should be avoided, but make sure the entire surface to be soldered is covered. After assembling the work the heated and tinned iron is dipped in the flux and held on the end of the stick of solder until some melts and sticks to the bit. Then the bit is held against the work so that it touches both pieces of metal comprising the joint, not just one. Hold the iron in place to permit the metal to be heated, and when the flux starts to boil, watch closely for the solder to start to flow off the iron as the work reaches its melting point. At this stage, slowly move the iron along the joint, allowing time for it to heat the work and the solder to be drawn into the joint by capillary action as it goes. When the solder on the bit has been used up, dip it in the flux again, pick up more solder and continue.

If the work does not seem to be heating up, check whether the bit of the iron is in fact touching both pieces of metal comprising the joint. Also check to see that there is a good surface area of the bit touching the work. Soldering irons heat the work by conduction and good surface contact is needed for this to take place. Dirt under the soldering iron can also prevent the metal-to-metal contact that is necessary for this.

It is possible to boil away the flux before the soldering iron reaches that part of the joint, allowing oxidation to occur before the solder takes to the metal. If this happens, the only solution is to re-clean and flux the work. When soldering re-starts, move the iron a little faster, or apply more flux while soldering proceeds.

Long seams may be soldered by applying more solder to the bit while it is still in place on the work, rather than keep removing it to pick up more solder. The latter procedure can lead to a blotchy and untidy joint.

Surplus solder is best removed from work by scrapers rather than files. It may be filed but, being soft, tends to rapidly clog the file. A hot soldering iron run over a cleaned up seam will smooth away file and scraper marks from the solder.

Some soldering work is aided if the two parts of the joint are tinned first.

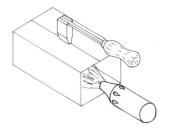

Fig. 98 *Using a blowlamp to provide back-up heat when soldering a seam on a large workpiece.*

This is often helpful when soft soldering steel components.

Sweating
Sweating is a variant of the soft soldering process, often used when very neat joints are required or when the joint comprises large surfaces. Both mating surfaces are tinned and fluxed. Then the two are held together and heated, either by a soldering iron or over a gentle flame, until the solder melts. This point may be recognised by small beads of solder oozing out at the edge of the joint, giving rise to the name applied to this technique.

Larger Items
When soft soldering large items such as tanks and car radiators, a soldering iron alone may be found to provide insufficient heat. The best way, then, is to use a torch or blowlamp to provide back-up heating. Pre-heat the work by playing the flame gently over the surface after the joint has been fluxed. When the work feels generally warm play the flame on the joint until the flux starts to melt or, in the case of liquid fluxes, to discolour. Then apply the solder with the soldering iron in the normal way, continuing gentle application of the flame. Extra flux may well be needed while this is taking place and should be coated on the work as necessary. It is best, for this sort of work, to stand or clamp the work securely as both hands will be fully occupied handling the tools and solder. An assistant is also a useful asset! Fig. 98 should convey the general idea.

The strongest soft soldered joints are those where the metals are as close fitting as possible with only the very smallest amount of solder separating them. Most of the strength of these joints comes from the alloy that is formed by the tin from the solder and the surface layers of the base metal. This is stronger than the soft solder itself and the point should be borne in mind when producing and designing joints.

Aluminium Solders

Aluminium has always been regarded as a difficult metal to solder and in many ways this is still true. There are now, however, several commercial solders and fluxes on the market designed for use with this metal and its alloys. Some are intended for use with a soldering iron and some for a torch. The important thing is to read and follow the manufacturer's instructions.

The soldering iron varieties seem to require a higher temperature than normal soft solders and this does restrict their usefulness.

The types intended for use with a torch seem to be more useful for the sort of work under consideration in this book. A danger is that the aluminium workpiece is very easily heated and melted during soldering as the melting point of these solders seems very close to that of the aluminium.

In my view, the conclusion must be that whilst it is now possible to solder aluminium in the average home workshops, it should not be considered an easy process.

Hard Soldering (General Comments)

As its name suggests, this is a stronger form of soldering than soft soldering. The principles upon which it works are, however, the same. It is the alloys used and the higher temperatures required that give rise to the main differences.

Hard soldering is stronger than soft and is frequently used for this reason. It may be correctly used where higher temperatures need to be withstood by the finished work. Also because it will give a closer fitting joint it can be used to give a neater job.

There are two kinds of hard soldering, known generally as silver soldering and brazing. Silver solders are alloys of copper, zinc and silver, basically, and melt between 700°C and 800°C. Brazing spelters are alloys of copper and zinc, therefore being types of brass and giving the process its name. They melt between 850°C and 950°C. From the point of view of producing a joint the only difference is that brazing needs higher temperature and fluxes to withstand them. The methods used are otherwise identical.

It is often stated that there are three grades of silver solder, easy (lowest melting point), medium and hard, but this is an over-simplification of the case. There are quite a number of different grades available.* What is true is that it is worth stocking types with three distinctly different melting points and keeping them clearly identified. In the type of work for which hard soldering is used, it is often necessary to solder separate joints in close proximity to one another at different times. The use of solder of lower melting points on the later joints reduces the risk of melting the earlier work. When choosing silver solders it is best to consult manufacturers or suppliers as to the most suitable types for the work proposed.

Some silver solders contain cadmium. There has recently been some concern over the effects on health of the

---

*See 'Soldering and Brazing', No. 9 in the Argus Workshop Practice series.

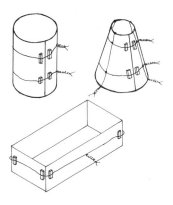

Fig. 99 *Common shapes wired together for hard soldering. Scrap metal packing prevents wire being soldered to joints.*

fumes given off when these are used. Such solders are probably best avoided or, at least, good ventilation ensured and care exercised when using them.

Borax is often quoted as the flux for hard soldering. While this may be used for some work, the position is not so simple as this. One danger in hard soldering is that because of the higher temperatures involved, the flux can be burnt away before the work is heated to the melting point of the solder. Therefore, materials are needed that will withstand prolonged heating and a flux should be used that suits the solder and base metal in use. The best advice is to choose the flux recommended by the manufacturer of the solder or spelter. A few hard solders may be found that do not require a flux (e.g. Johnson Matthey's Silbralloy, no flux on copper) but this is unusual.

Hard soldering fluxes are usually in powder form. If applied to the work like this, they will be blown away by the torch flame before they melt. The usual method is to mix them into a paste with

a little water before applying them to the work.

Hard solders are not so easy to obtain as soft solders, which are often stocked by the high street ironmonger. One of the better known manufacturers is Johnson Matthey and Co., of Hatton Garden, whose specifications are often quoted in books and magazine articles. Engineers' and welders' suppliers often stock them as do many of the firms advertising in *Model Engineer* and other similar publications.

Procedure

The process of hard soldering is often regarded with suspicion by amateurs or beginners. This is a shame as it is stronger, and in many ways easier, than soft soldering. So long as the correct solder and flux are used, together with a heating set up that will achieve the required temperature fairly quickly, there should not be any problem.

First prepare and assemble the work. Joints should be really close fitting and clean with flux applied before assembly. Remember that hard solders flow very freely and will tend to run wherever the flux is. The placing of flux should be carried out carefully to avoid a workpiece whose surface is covered with solder runs. Jeweller's rouge paste may also be used to restrict the solder to the places where it is needed.

After assembly, the parts being soldered will need to be held together. It is no good relying on the natural fit of the parts as expansion during heating, and the pressures of boiling flux, can force them apart. Some work can be weighted down with pieces of firebrick or held with clamps, but usually iron binding wire is used to hold work together during the soldering operation. The usual way in which common shapes are held with wire is shown in Fig. 99. Care needs to be taken not to melt this wire with the torch.

The next step is to set the work up on a firebrick or other heat resistant and non-conductive surface. This should be done in such a way that the torch flame can get to both sides of the joint. Do not try to work with one side of the joint in contact with the bricks. Further firebricks should be placed around the work, but not touching it, to reflect the heat on to it.

Snippings of solder may be placed at intervals along the line of the joint which is then heated by the torch until they melt and flow. It is unlikely, unless the work is small, that the whole joint will be brought to the correct temperature in one go. Therefore, it is necessary to move the flame along the work as the solder melts. As the heat moves along the joint, the solder melts and flows with it. Continue like this until the whole joint is soldered, but do not continue heating after the solder has flowed into the joint. The work may then be allowed to cool after which cleaning can commence. Some work can be cooled by quenching, but be cautious over this as distortion can be caused. All work must be left long enough for the solder to solidify before it is moved.

It is not essential to place small pieces of solder along the joint, as described above. Many people prefer to heat the joint with the flame until the melting point of the solder is reached. A stick of solder is held in the hand and moved in and out of the flame to warm it during the heating of the work. As soon as the work is hot enough the end of the stick of solder is gently touched on the open edge of the joint. If everything has been correctly judged, the end of the solder will melt and be drawn into the joint by

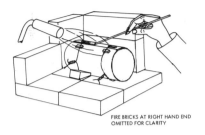

FIRE BRICKS AT RIGHT HAND END OMITTED FOR CLARITY

Fig. 100 *Hard soldering in progress. Solder will always flow towards the heated area.*

capillary action. Continue heating and applying solder along the length of the joint. The temperature of the work may be judged both by the colour of the metal and that of the flux. For low melting point silver solders, a dull red heat is usually sufficient. At this temperature, the flux will first have dried and hardened to a white colour during the early stages of heating, followed by melting to a colourless liquid of sticky consistency. At this point the work is ready for the solder to be applied. For higher melting point silver solders a good red heat is needed and for brazing spelters, bright red/orange heat.

Of the two methods, the first is probably easier for beginners and less experienced workers since the solder will tell when its melting point has been reached. The second method can save time and avoids the problem of estimating the amount of solder the joint will consume. This is not always as easy as it may seem and usually one tends to err on the high side to make certain of the job. Messy and untidy work can result from over-estimation. The best advice, in my opinion, is to try both methods to see which is the most suited to one's own practice. Generally,

101

though, I have found that both methods are needed from time to time. Some jobs 'feel' more suited to the first and some to the second. Experience is the best guide here.

In all hard soldering work, the joint should be brought to the soldering heat as quickly as possible. Prolonged heating can cause even the correct fluxes to be burnt away, and this often seems to be the cause of failure in this process. If this happens, it can be recognised by blackening of the line of the joint and the flux and an unwillingness of the solder to flow, even when melted. The only solution is to clean the work, re-flux and start again.

Brazing
The procedure for brazing is the same as for silver soldering, but make sure the correct flux is used. Because of the higher temperatures required, the average gas/air or bottled gas torch is working at, or near, its limit for this work. It is, therefore, essential for the work to be surrounded by firebricks etc, so that as little heat as possible is allowed to escape. Oxy-acetylene or similar equipment, with its much higher temperatures, makes this work easy from the point of view of attaining the necessary temperature.

Sif-bronze Welding
Sif-bronze welding is a form of brazing developed by the firm of S.I.F. who manufacture many kinds of welding and brazing materials. It is intended for use with oxy-acetylene equipment but may, in fact, be used with any heating method that will bring the work to a bright red/orange heat. In my own experience it is less strong than welding but is quite good for making up steel fabrications, while it will also work for other metals like monel and copper. It has better gap-filling ability than other hard solders I have used but does not seem to penetrate joints so well.

Suspicions of possible occasional adverse reaction to the products of coal combustion, together with the apparent lesser penetration, have led some experienced model engineers to suggest caution in using this material in coal-fired boilers; no doubt the makers can advise.

Using Sif-bronze is easier than other hard solders, so long as the required temperature may be attained. This is largely the result of the flux used, which is specially made for the job, and has a very good cleaning effect. The work is heated to a bright red heat and the end of the brazing rod is heated in the flame. Whilst hot, the rod is then dipped in the flux powder, some of which sticks to it. This is then touched gently on the joint and the heat from the metal allowed to melt first the flux, then the brazing rod. The heat is moved progressively along the joint applying more flux and spelter as necessary until the whole joint has been brazed.

With this system, the metal does not need to be so clean, as the flux will lift oxide and even light rust and dirt from the surface. It will even work on black steel and is, therefore, very useful for repair work or where access for cleaning is difficult. The flux residue is, however, very hard and can be difficult to remove.

Final Comments
Brass may be silver soldered, but not brazed, since it melts at, or near, the same temperature as many brazing alloys.

For the same reason, metals of low melting point like lead, aluminium and zinc may not be hard soldered at all.

CHAPTER 7

Rivets and Riveting

Rivets are short pieces of metal rod which have a head, or swollen portion, on one end. They are placed through aligning holes in the metals being joined and a second head is formed on the other end, so holding the two, or more, pieces of metal together. In the smaller sizes, with which we are concered here, rivet heads are usually formed cold by a hammering or pressing process. It follows, therefore, that rivets need to be made from metals which are soft and malleable by nature and to be in their softened, or annealed, state when ready for use.

In sheet metalwork, the use of rivets is far less common than at one time. The considerable expansion of welding technology has largely been responsible for this. For home workshop use, and in one-off work, they do still possess a number of advantages, however. Not least is the fact that a riveted joint may be produced with comparatively simple equipment. It may also be produced entirely by hand, if necessary, when no power is available.

Further advantages attached to using rivets are that it is possible to remove the rivets if dismantling is necessary. Also, because no heat is used or struc-tural changes made to metals joined by riveting, distortion is kept to a minimum and metals of low melting point are not put at risk.

One other reason for using rivets, that may well apply to readers of this book, is when modelling a prototype with visible rivet heads.

Rivets, therefore, are a useful means of joining sheet metal for the type of work described here. They may find uses in very many situations and it is worth acquiring some knowledge of riveting techniques.

Specialist Tools Required

Apart from the normal metalworking tools mentioned in other sections of this book, a few simple but important tools are required for work with rivets. The most important are sets and snaps for the size and type of rivets in use. Some examples of these are shown in Fig. 101. Both types may be bought, although the combined set and snap is the one that is traditionally commercially produced. The single type are quite easy to make at home, especially if a lathe is available. Ideally, but not essentially, they should be hardened and tempered, or case-hardened.

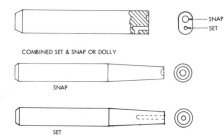

COMBINED SET & SNAP OR DOLLY

SNAP

SET

Fig. 101 *Rivet sets and snaps.*

For a long time after I started metal-working I puzzled over how to make the half-round depressions usually required in rivet snaps. Embossing them with the metal at red heat, using a suitable size bearing ball, is sometimes recommended, but the easiest way found, so far, is to use a drill. One of the same diameter as the rivet head is selected and the point modified by grinding to a curved rather than angular shape. If a pilot hole of the correct depth is drilled, it may be opened out to shape and diameter using the re-ground drill.

The ends of single rivet sets and snaps should be tapered so that they can work as close to shoulders as possible. Much riveting seems to take place near the edges of components, and it is often necessary to grind or file away parts of rivet sets and snaps to get them into these locations. This is often the case when riveting angle section metal to the edges of flat plates for joining or stiffening.

A shortage of hands to hold work and tools is often a problem when riveting. Supports, stands, clamps and packing of various heights and sizes are, therefore, useful. Wooden boxes and trestles can be used to support long work over-hanging the bench. There are many situations of this kind where work

needs dealing with on an individual basis.

An essential tool for most riveting is a hammer, and the engineer's ball pein hammer is the one to choose. A good general purpose size is ¾lb or 1lb. The basic shaping of rivet heads is carried out with the ball pein, rather than the flat face of the hammer. This restricts the effect of the hammer to one spot, permitting the exact placing of each hammer blow to control the shaping process.

Punches of various types can be of use. The centre punch is, of course, needed for marking out for drilling, but flat ended parallel pin punches and drifts are also useful for removing rivets when necessary. They do have another use. Sometimes, when working in corners and near edges it becomes impossible to make the hammer head reach the rivet. A cross-pein hammer may work, but usually the only way is to rest the punch on the rivet and hammer the punch, moving it around as necessary to control the shaping. This may sound like a bodge, but I have known occasions when there was no other way to form the rivet head and it can be made to produce adequate results.

Rivets often need trimming to length before the second head may be formed. They can be marked, removed from the work and cut with a junior hacksaw, but this is time consuming and laborious. A better way is to snip them to length in situ using suitable cutters. One is soon able to judge the lengths of shank required and to snip off any surplus metal. Pliers will do this job but with rivets over 2mm (³⁄₃₂″) diameter they become rather hard work. Toggle jointed end cutting pincher-type cutters are the best for this job. Remember to keep the face and eyes out of the way

104

when cutting off rivets like this, as the cut piece tends to fly out at high speed.

Pop riveting is mentioned in detail later on. If this type of riveting is planned, a set of pop riveting pliers or tongs will be essential.

Rivet Types

Rivets are usually described according to the shape of the head with which they are supplied. Their size is measured by their diameter and length. For most rivets, the length quoted is that of the shank, but the length of a countersunk rivet includes the head. In addition, the metal from which a rivet is made needs to be given, in order to describe it fully.

Soft iron, copper, aluminium alloy and mild steel are the metals in which rivets may most frequently be obtained. Brass, monel and other less common metals are also used, however, for making rivets. To avoid corrosion problems, the rivets should be made of the same metal as that being joined.

The types of rivets of most use for the work described in this book are illustrated in Fig. 102. Round, or snap head rivets may be considered as the general purpose kind. Countersunk (CSK) rivets are used when a flush surface is needed, the same as countersunk screws. There are three different angles applied to the heads of countersunk rivets. The standard is 90° included. This is the general purpose one, whilst 60° is for thicker metal to give greater strength, and 120° is for thinner work. The larger area of the head spreads the load and means that the countersunk drill is less likely to start enlarging the hole. The standard ones will, however, be found to be satisfactory for most work. Flat head rivets are often called tinman's rivets and are, again, intended

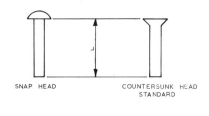

SNAP HEAD   COUNTERSUNK HEAD STANDARD

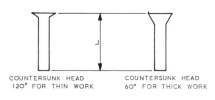

COUNTERSUNK HEAD 120° FOR THIN WORK   COUNTERSUNK HEAD 60° FOR THICK WORK

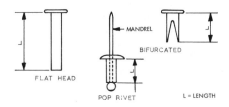

FLAT HEAD   MANDREL   BIFURCATED   POP RIVET   L = LENGTH

Fig. 102 *Rivet types.*

for use with thin metal. Bifurcated rivets are used when joining a non-metallic material, like felt or leather to metal. Pop rivets are used when there is only access from one side or when a quick job is required. Their strength is inferior to that of the traditional rivets, however, and they are not really liquid or gas-tight.

Any shape of rivet, except the pop or bifurcated ones, may have a head of any other shape formed on the plain end. Thus a snap head rivet may have a countersunk head formed on the other end and vice-versa. One frequently encounters situations of this kind.

105

Using Engineer's Rivets – Snap Head

Assuming a snap head rivet requires a similar head forming on its other end to close the joint, the procedure is as follows.

First, a hole needs to be drilled, equal to the shank diameter of the rivet, through both pieces of metal to be joined. After de-burring, the rivet is pushed through the holes in both pieces of metal which are then pressed tightly together using a rivet set as in Fig. 103(a). The formed head of the rivet should be supported in a snap, held in the vice as shown.

The shank of the rivet may next be cut off to length with pliers, cutters or junior hacksaw. No exact rule can be given about the length of shank required to form the second head. For a snap head, it is often quoted as being an amount equal to the rivet diameter and this is a good guide. However, the exact amount required depends upon

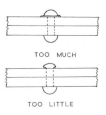

TOO MUCH

TOO LITTLE

Fig. 104 *Effect of allowing an incorrect amount of shank for forming the second head.*

the size of the snap being used. There should be enough shank left to completely fill the snap. Too little and a part-formed head will result. Too much and the finished head will have a 'collar' around the base. Both of these situations lead to a weaker joint. If the rivet snap in use has not been used before, it is wise to experiment on some scrap material to find the exact amount of shank to leave on the rivet.

Once the rivet has been cut to length, use the set again, then the forming of the second head can start. This is done using the flat face of the hammer, as in Fig. 103(b). Apart from starting the head, this is important because it expands the shank of the rivet to be a tight fit in the hole. Loose fitting rivet shanks allow the plates to 'work'. This has been known to cut through rivet shanks be exerting a shearing action.

The last stage is to roughly form the shape of the head using the ball pein of the hammer and to finish it with the second rivet snap, as in Fig. 103(c) and (d).

Lines of Rivets

Rivets are seldom used singly, a line, or two or more parallel lines of rivets being more usual. It is, of course, essential that the holes in both pieces of metal being riveted together match up exactly. Because the holes have to be a

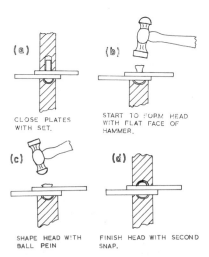

(a) CLOSE PLATES WITH SET.

(b) START TO FORM HEAD WITH FLAT FACE OF HAMMER.

(c) SHAPE HEAD WITH BALL PEIN

(d) FINISH HEAD WITH SECOND SNAP.

Fig. 103 *Forming a snap head.*

close fit on the rivet shanks, any slight errors in their alignment will prevent rivets passing through both pieces. Drilling and other working methods must be used, therefore, that will ensure an exact match of the holes in each side of the joint.

The normal method for smaller jobs where two pieces of metal are being joined together is to mark and drill all the holes in one piece. This is then offered up to, and correctly aligned with the second piece and one hole marked through. Any convenient and accurate method will do, but my own favourite is to put the drill through the existing hole and twist it backwards and forwards with the fingers. A mark is made by the drill point which may then be centre-punched and drilled.

Both pieces of metal may now be joined with one rivet. A second hole may then be drilled by working through another of the existing holes. This is then riveted. The other holes then follow, taking care to ensure that both pieces of metal are tightly held together during drilling. If they are not, burrs and swarf (shavings) can build up between the joint which will prevent close contact of both pieces of metal. This will cause weak or deformed joints.

A good way to hold a long joint is to drill and bolt together at intervals along the joint. Then drill and rivet between the bolts. Finally remove the bolts and replace them by rivets. Obviously bolts the same size or smaller than the rivets in use are needed. If smaller, the holes can be drilled out, one at a time, to rivet diameter, when ready.

Where the line of rivets is long, or the metal being riveted is soft, account has to be taken of the fact that the metal may spread slightly by the effect of the hammering used to form the rivets. In this case, the procedure is as described for the first two rivets, but the others must be drilled and riveted a few at a time, equally spaced along the line. A good method is to do every alternate rivet, or every third one along the line first. Then follow with the others.

Whenever possible it is best to leave final filing and fitting until after riveting to ensure accurate alignment of edges. If this is not possible, it is best to use clamps (toolmaker's clamps are ideal) to hold the work together while drilling and riveting the first few holes.

Countersunk Head

Metals to be joined by countersunk rivets must first be prepared by drilling, as for other types, except, of course, that the holes must be countersunk as well. One or both sides may be countersunk. If only one side, it is best to use rivets with the other head already formed, making the countersunk head when the rivet is in the work. Counter-

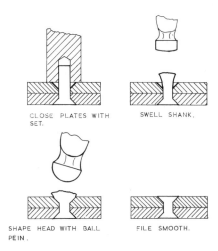

CLOSE PLATES WITH SET.

SWELL SHANK.

SHAPE HEAD WITH BALL PEIN.

FILE SMOOTH.

Fig. 105 *Forming a countersunk rivet head.*

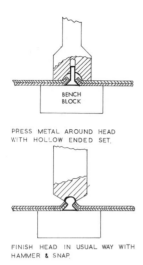

PRESS METAL AROUND HEAD
WITH HOLLOW ENDED SET

FINISH HEAD IN USUAL WAY WITH
HAMMER & SNAP

Fig. 106 *Countersunk rivets in thin sheet.*

sunk heads tend to be easier to form than other types.

After drilling the metals to be joined, a rivet is inserted and the two pieces of metal pressed together using a rivet set. Next, the shank is cut to length, allowing a little more material than for a snap head. Diameter x 1½ is commonly advised, but this is partly dependent on the size of the countersink, so it is wise to be prepared to modify this figure to suit the work. The countersink must be slightly over-filled, but no more, by the rivet shank after hammering.

When the rivet is cut to length, again use the set to ensure close contact between both pieces of metal comprising the joint. Then, using the flat face of the hammer, hit the end of the rivet to swell the shank. Follow this by using the ball pein to knock the rivet shank down into the countersunk hole and swell it until the hole is completely filled. Be prepared to place the hammer blows on different parts of the rivet as appears to

be required by the work as it proceeds.

Finally, the rivet is filed until it is completely flush with the surface of the work. If this is followed by the use of draw filing and emery cloth and the rivet head has completely filled the countersink, it should be invisible, or nearly so. As a guide to the ideal appearance of a countersunk riveted joint, look at the point where the blade and stock of an engineer's try-square are joined. Between three and five countersunk rivets are usually used for this. Try to find them!

Countersunk heads are not so strong as other types and are usually used when an unobstructed surface is needed. Sometimes they are used because they are easier to form. As with other rivets their strength is seriously reduced if the heads are badly formed. Most faults of this kind are caused either by incorrect size countersinks, or too much, or too little shank being allowed for forming the head. It is usually best, especially when starting, to make countersinks slightly under their theoretically correct size (2 x hole dia.) when they are for riveting. In theory, this produces a weaker joint since the head of the rivet is smaller than ideal. In practice, I have found that it is more likely to result in a countersink filled by the rivet. This is stronger than a correct size countersink only partly filled by a poorly formed rivet, or one where the shank has bent over during forming.

When working with very thin metal, as may often be the case with sheet metalwork, it can be found that there is not sufficient thickness of metal to permit satisfactory countersinking. If countersunk rivets must be used in a situation of this sort, the method shown in Fig. 106 can be adopted. Here, both pieces of metal are drilled, but not countersunk, and a countersunk rivet is placed through. The countersunk head is rested on a flat metal surface and a special set, of the type shown, is used. This has the effect of sinking the rivet head into the metal. A normal head may then be formed with hammer and snap on the other side. If it is then soldered on both sides it may be made liquid-tight and can, for this reason, find use in the construction of small tanks and cans.

Where lines of countersunk rivets are needed the requirements for accurate alignment of holes, and the methods used to achieve this, are the same as described for snap head rivets. Indeed, these methods apply whatever shape of rivet heads may be in use.

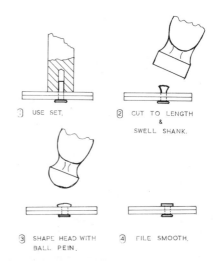

① USE SET.

② CUT TO LENGTH
& SWELL SHANK.

③ SHAPE HEAD WITH BALL PEIN.

④ FILE SMOOTH.

Fig. 107 *Forming a flat head.*

Flat Head
Flat head rivets may be treated in the way shown in Fig. 107. The formed head is rested on a flat metal surface (not the vice slide!), the set used and the shank cut to length as for a snap head. The flat face of the hammer is then used to swell the shank and the ball pein to roughly shape the head. No snap is used, the top of the head being flattened by a few file strokes.

Size of Holes for Rivets
A hole to take a rivet should be slightly larger than the shank diameter. During riveting the shank is swelled to become a tight fit in the hole. It may be thought, therefore, that a drill slightly larger than shank diameter must be used, and in larger sizes this is often done. Indeed, figures are published quoting exact limits for over-size holes.

For the sort and size of work required by most model engineers and amateurs, however, it is not necessary to worry about this. A normal twist drill makes a hole slightly larger than its nominal diameter and this gives sufficient clearance for most small and medium size riveting work. Therefore, it is simply necessary to choose a drill whose stated diameter is the same as that of the shank of the rivet in use.

Pop Rivets
These are sometimes called blind rivets, but this is incorrect as there is another type of rivet which uses this name. Pop rivets are a very quick and useful way of joining sheet metal for light, non-liquid tight items. They are most usually made from aluminium alloy with a mushroom head, but ones made from other metals and countersunk headed varieties may also be obtained.

If the drawing of the pop rivet in Fig. 102 is studied it will be seen that it consists of two separate parts, the rivet proper and the mandrel. Just inside the plain end of the rivet, the diameter of a short length of the mandrel is reduced so that it forms a weak portion. In use, the rivet is placed through both pieces of metal joined, which must be drilled to suit the rivet, as for other forms of riveting. The outer end of the mandrel is gripped by the collets in a special pair of pliers. Operating the pliers pulls the mandrel upwards, while pressing the rivet firmly into place and causing the shank to be swelled by pressure from the large end of the mandrel. When sufficient pressure has been exerted to swell the shank by the correct amount, the mandrel snaps off at its weak point, leaving the rivet in place. In practice, this process takes no more than a few seconds for each rivet.

Pop rivets can be formed by working from one side of the metal only and are, therefore, useful in situations where there is no access to one surface. This was, originally, their intended use in the aircraft industry, but they have many applications in all kinds of general metalwork. They are very useful when fixing to tubes such as aluminium alloy boat masts, or fixing sheets to tubular frameworks. Apart from this they are useful because of their speed and simplicity of use in all kinds of sheet metal constructions.

Pop riveting pliers are fairly widely available from D.I.Y. shops and other tool suppliers. There are many different designs on the market, quite reasonably priced. Because of this and their easy use, pop rivets are an ideal fastening device for the home metalworker. However, they do have some disadvantages which need to be borne in mind. Firstly, they are not so strong as other types of rivet and should not be used in heavy duty, load bearing situations. To a certain extent their weaker nature may be overcome by increasing the number of rivets used, compared to other types, but scope for doing this is limited. Secondly, they are not liquid or gas tight because they are hollow. Filler paste can be used to waterproof them if used for some work but they would not, for example, be of use for assembling any kind of pressurised container. Finally, they are most frequently available made from aluminium or its alloys. If used with other metals they can cause more rapid corrosion, especially in the presence of water or chemicals. It depends upon the use to which the item being made will be put. Sometimes paint will form sufficient protection for the corrosion factor to be safely ignored. As an example to illustrate the point I am attempting to make, it would be wrong to assemble brass water tanks for a model steam locomotive with pop rivets, but a tool box made from thin steel sheet could be held together with them quite happily.

Removing Rivets

One advantage of rivets is that they can be removed, allowing the pieces of metal joined to be separated, without any damage to their structure.

The traditional method is to centre punch the rivet head at its centre and drill in with a drill the same diameter as the rivet shank. This either makes the head fall off or permits its easy removal with a cold chisel. A pin punch or drift may then be used to knock the rivet out, with the work supported from underneath around the other rivet head. Pop rivets are very easily removed by this method, but do not, of course, need centre punching. It is usually described as 'drilling out'.

It is not always easy to make the drilled hole come sufficiently close to the centre of the rivet head to remove it.

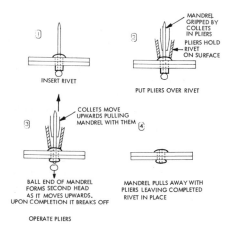

INSERT RIVET

PUT PLIERS OVER RIVET

MANDREL GRIPPED BY COLLETS IN PLIERS

PLIERS HOLD RIVET ON SURFACE

COLLETS MOVE UPWARDS PULLING MANDREL WITH THEM

BALL END OF MANDREL FORMS SECOND HEAD AS IT MOVES UPWARDS. UPON COMPLETION IT BREAKS OFF

OPERATE PLIERS

MANDREL PULLS AWAY WITH PLIERS LEAVING COMPLETED RIVET IN PLACE

Fig. 108 *Forming pop rivets.*

Also, if care is not taken over the depth of the hole, the work can be damaged. For these reasons it may be better, if possible, to file, chisel or grind away the rivet head from one side of the work. Small grinding discs running in portable power drills are quite good for this work. The rivet may then be punched out, as before.

Sometimes it is possible to use a junior hacksaw to cut away the rivet head and large rivets can have their heads burned away with an oxyacetylene cutting torch.

Countersunk heads are a little more difficult to deal with. For this reason, where one head is of another type, it is best to remove this one. If a countersunk head must be removed, it is probably best to centre punch as near to its centre as can be judged and drill a hole of shank diameter to the same depth as the head. This should make the head part company with the shank, but will not if it is not accurately centred. In this case, the hole should gradually be enlarged with a countersink drill until it is found possible to punch the rivet out. This enlarging could, alternatively, be performed by a small burr held in a flexible drive from a power tool.

Removing rivets is not the easiest of tasks but neither is it one of the most difficult. When separating items for repair work to take place, they can be easier to deal with than rusted nuts and bolts. It is certainly easier to separate, and later re-make, a riveted joint than one made by welding or hard soldering.

Hold-Ups and Special Purpose Rivet Snaps

Riveting work often has to be carried out on parts of the work where access for the riveting tools is difficult. It is, for example, impossible to use an ordinary rivet snap inside the central areas of tanks and other containers. When riveting long seams on such articles, the device illustrated in Fig. 109(a) may be used. Its size should be substantial compared to the work and the outer support could be adjustable for height, but must be firm.

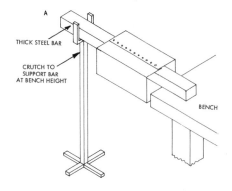

THICK STEEL BAR

CRUTCH TO SUPPORT BAR AT BENCH HEIGHT

A

BENCH

Fig. 109a *Riveting large or awkward work.*

111

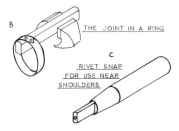

THE JOINT IN A RING

RIVET SNAP
FOR USE NEAR
SHOULDERS

B

C

Fig. 109b and c

Where the ends of hoops and rings have to be joined by riveting, a special rivet snap can be made that will fit in the vice as in Fig 109(b). Note that this should not be just a flat bar, it should have a recess shaped to match the rivet head like any other rivet snap. If not, flattened and spoiled rivet heads will result on the inside surface of the work.

The same snap, if the cup to accept the rivet head is as close as possible to the end, may be used when riveting near edges and shoulders, or on the inside surfaces of angle section metal. If making up such a tool, it is worth making different size snaps at each end of each flat surface. This will permit its use with a variety of sizes of rivets.

Fig. 109(c) shows a rivet set with cut away sides. This is also to allow work close to edges, or close to other rivets.

The tool shown in Fig. 110 is designed as a snap or hold up for use in

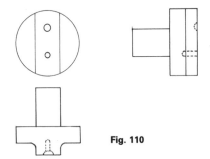

Fig. 110

combination with the tool in Fig. 109(b), or for holding in an anvil. It may be fitted into a hole drilled in the bar. A number of holes will permit it to be moved about to suit the work in hand. Different size snaps can be made up to allow work with different size rivets.

All the tools described must be substantial in size in relation to the work and rivets with which they are intended to be used. Since this will vary no further rules over dimensions can be given. All snaps and hold-ups for use in the vice should be given a sufficiently long shank to rest on the vice slide, or shoulders to rest on the jaws. If not,

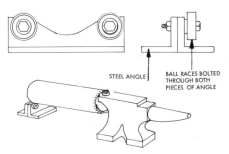

STEEL ANGLE

BALL RACES BOLTED
THROUGH BOTH
PIECES OF ANGLE

Fig. 111 *Device for supporting long circular work during riveting.*

they will be progressively pushed downwards when the rivet is hammered, no matter how tightly the vice is closed.

Some jobs are awkward to rivet by virtue of their size and shape. It is often worth giving some thought to ways of supporting such work, especially if an assistant is not available. The device and set-up shown in Fig. 111 are for riveting a recessed end cap to a cylindrical work-piece. It is the sort of situation that may be encountered in model boiler making work. To support the cylinder, the device shown can be made from a couple of off-cuts of angle or a piece of T section, if available. A block of wood may also suffice. The ball races bolted to it take the weight of the work and allow it to be easily revolved during riveting. A snap, or hold up, to go under the rivet is shown resting on a small bench anvil, but, in the absence of one of these, metal packing or a vice could be used. The snap is the same as the one illustrated in Fig. 110, the cut away sides allowing for the curve of the cylinder.

If only one or two rivets need to be dealt with, it may not be considered worth the trouble of making up some of the tools or equipment described here. In this case, if working with iron or mild steel rivets a piece of aluminium upwards of 3mm (⅛″) thick may be used in place of the supporting snap. Being fairly soft it will not flatten the rivet head, but will allow it to become slightly embossed into its surface. I have used this method with success when riveting pieces of small angle section on to the ends of strips. The work was held in the vice so that the bottom rivet head rested on the top of an aluminium vice clam.

This will not suit all work, and, often, suitable tools will have to be made up. Usually it is worth doing this as such items nearly always seem to find a use in future work, not just in the job for which they were made. Remember that the surfaces of special hold-ups and snaps only need hollows in them if working with snap head rivets. Countersunk and flat head rivets only need a flat surface on which to rest.

Size and Spacing of Rivets

Although there are certain well-established rules pertaining to this sub-

ject, it must first be pointed out that it will often not be possible to keep to them exactly. Rivets are made in standard sizes and because they are often needed in some quantity it is not, usually, sensible to make them oneself. The procedure is to work out the ideal size required then choose the nearest size available, usually above that of the theoretical requirement. If forced to use rivets smaller than ideal, then the number used may be increased. Much depends upon the use to which the finished work will be put. Some com-

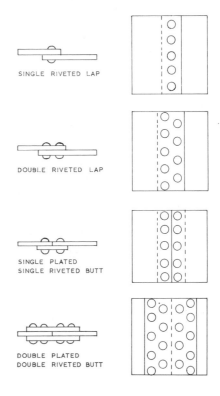

SINGLE RIVETED LAP

DOUBLE RIVETED LAP

SINGLE PLATED
SINGLE RIVETED BUTT

DOUBLE PLATED
DOUBLE RIVETED BUTT

Fig. 112 *Rivet layouts.*

113

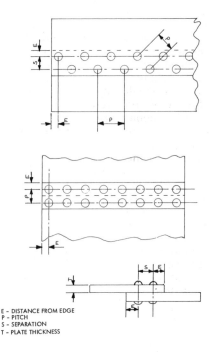

E – DISTANCE FROM EDGE
P – PITCH
S – SEPARATION
T – PLATE THICKNESS

Fig. 113 *Rivet spacing.*

monly used standard layouts and joints
are shown in Fig. 112.

The standard dimensions and spacing rules are as follows:-

Diameter of rivet = 1.2 to 1.5 × plate
    thickness
Edge of hole centre to edges of plate =
    1.5 × rivet diameter
Pitch of rivets = 3 × rivet diameter
Separation of rows of rivets = 2 × rivet
    diameter

Fig. 113 should help to make the
meaning of these terms clear, and remember that some flexibility is needed
in their application.

CHAPTER 8

Welding

Although rapid advances in welding technology have been made during the last 20 to 30 years, the equipment that is normally available for home use is not the ideal type for dealing with thin metal sheet. The problems in dealing with this material are distortion and the likelihood of burning holes. While welding equipment is available to cope easily with this sort of work, it will, for the time being at least, be beyond the means of the average amateur metalworker.

Having said this, there is a place for the use of welding in home sheet metalwork, especially when using steel in the thicker sizes. The eventual acquisition of welding equipment, with its usefulness for other types of work, is not likely to be regretted. Just do not expect too much of it: the uninitiated often seem to regard welding as the answer to every problem of joining metals. It is not.

The most easily and frequently welded metal is mild steel, closely followed by other types of steel. Other metals may also be welded, some more easily than others. In all cases, though, the meaning of the term 'welding' is the same. A properly welded joint will consist of the same metal throughout, the edges of both pieces being joined having been melted and more metal of the same type run into the molten pool. When solidified, such a joint is nearly as strong as if it had been made from one piece of metal. As with other processes, the more the ideal is departed from, the weaker the joint.

Welding Equipment – Oxy-acetylene
In many ways this is the best type of equipment for a variety of small welding tasks. It is versatile and independent of any kind of power supply, except for the cylinders containing the gases. Apart from welding oxy-acetylene equipment can be used for brazing and easily attains the higher temperatures required for this. It may be used for other forms of soldering and as a general heat source, although this would be rather extravagent.

Oxy-acetylene, or gas welding, derives its title from the fact that a flame composed of oxygen and acetylene gases is used as the heat source. The acetylene burns in the oxygen which allows it to reach a temperature in excess of 3000°C. The proportions of the gases may be varied to give the different types of flames needed for different types of work. Larger and small nozzles may be used to vary the size of flame to suit the size of the work.

The oxygen and acetylene gases are contained in separate cylinders, colour coded black for oxygen and maroon for acetylene. Pressure regulators with manually operated controls feed each gas via flame traps and non-return valves through hoses to the torch. Gauges indicate the supply pressure and the pressure of gas remaining in each cylinder. Valves on the torch control the amount of gas supplied to the flame via the nozzle which is screwed into the handle of the torch. Probably the best known manufacturer of gas welding equipment is the British Oxygen Company, although there are other, quite reputable, firms producing equipment of equal quality. Most fittings and threaded components are standardised, although there is more than one standard size. Care must, therefore, be taken to ensure that sizes of torches, hoses, gauges etc, are matched. Gauge fittings to cylinders are standardised with right hand threads for oxygen and left hand for acetylene. This rule is also followed with all other fittings on torches and hoses.

The usual situation with oxy-acetylene equipment is that the user owns the torch, gauges, pressure regulators, etc and hires the gas cylinders, which remain the property of the supplier. Only the gas contained in the cylinders is owned by the user who pays for it when supplied.

Gas cylinders require a certain amount of care in handling and storage. They should not be kept in wooden or other potentially inflammable shed-type buildings and must be kept standing up. Acetylene cylinders become especially dangerous if used while, or shortly after, being laid down. They must not be used if the pressure of gas remaining in them has dropped below 10lb per square inch. Oxygen, its cylinders and all fittings and pressure gauges, must never come into contact with any oil. They should be stored well away from this.

While using an oxy-acetylene torch, tinted goggles must be worn to protect the eyes from the bright light of the flame.

Various sizes of gas cylinders are available. Those most usually encountered stand around 1.5 metres (5ft) high and are rather heavy to handle. Smaller size cylinders are available and, while less economical, they are much more portable. A welding set using these small portable cylinders with a standard torch and pressure regulators will do the same work as one with the large size cylinders. The period of use between cylinder replacement will, however, be much shorter, but may be acceptable when only a small amount of work is to be undertaken.

For the normal run of work done by the amateur sheet metalworker, oxy-acetylene is probably the ideal welding system to use. Unfortunately, cylinder rental and gas prices are fairly high, and rental charges must be paid whether the equipment is used or not. Together with the storage requirements, the majority of people will probably decide that this makes it an unacceptable welding system for home use. Torches and pressure regulators are also quite expensive items, but if the storage facilities exist and the money is available, oxy-acetylene welding equipment is highly desirable.

Electric Arc Welding Equipment
The range of electric arc welding equip-

116

ment now available is very large and a full description of it would take up most of this book. It is, probably, the area of welding in which most of the developments of more recent years have been made.

For arc welding, the basic item of equipment is a heavy duty transformer. This is often called a 'welding set', and most frequently works from the mains electricity supply. Some welding sets incorporate their own petrol or diesel generator and some are designed to work from car batteries.

Industrial welding transformers can consume as much, or more, electricity as the whole of an average household and are not, therefore, very suitable for home use. Fortunately, there are several reasonably priced makes of small transformers available designed to work from a 13 amp domestic power point. These are frequently advertised in publications like *Exchange and Mart*, the various motoring magazines and *Model Engineer*. They can be either of two types. Oil cooled ones tend to be more expensive, but are capable of long, heavy continuous use. Air cooled variants can sometimes overheat during long jobs, but are cheaper. They are usually fitted with thermal cut-outs and if these trip, it is a simple matter of waiting until things have cooled down before resuming work. Air cooled transformers are quite adequate for normal home welding work.

The task of the welding transformer is to reduce the mains voltage and so increase the current (amps) available to a level suitable for welding. Comparatively low voltages are needed, it is the amps which do the welding and which are used to describe the size of a welding transformer. Thus, a 140 amp welding set is one in which up to 140 amps

are available at the weld, not one which takes 140 amps from the mains. The thicker the metal being welded the greater the current required.

When choosing a welding transformer, apart from the obvious requirements of quality and electrical safety, it is important to consider the size in relation to the work to be undertaken. Suppliers and manufacturers will usually give advice as to the capabilities of particular sets. It is better to have one a little larger than required so that it is not normally being asked for its maximum output. About 90 to 140 amps seem to be the most useful sizes of welding sets for home use.

As well as a transformer, certain other equipment is needed before arc welding can proceed. An electrode holder is needed to hold the electrode, or welding rod. An earthing clamp is required to connect to the work and both these items need reasonable lengths of heavy cable to connect then to the terminals on the transformer. Correct flux coated welding rods, or electrodes, are needed in fairly generous quantities. They must be of a suitable thickness for the work in hand and must consist of the same metal. Electrodes can be bought singly or in tens, but it is much more economical, if possible, to buy them in packets of a hundred or so. If stored in a dry place they have an indefinite shelf life. The other essential item is a face mask and this must be of the correct type. Arc welding gives off intense ultra-violet light which will harm the eyes unless viewed through a proper filter. Welding masks contain such a filter through which the work can be safely watched while welding. They also cover the face and protect it from the 'sunburn' that can be caused by the u.v. light. A chipping hammer to remove slag after welding, and a wire brush for preparatory cleaning work will be useful but can be managed without.

All the above items can be obtained separately from transformers but usually they are included in the price with ones aimed at the home market. Electrodes will be the item one most frequently needs to buy separately. As with the other equipment mentioned, they may be obtained from the better tool shops and from specialist welding suppliers.

Electric arc welding is less versatile and controllable than gas welding. It may be used, with care, on thin metal, but is much more at home when working with metal of 2mm (3/32 inch) thickness and upwards. It is much quicker than gas welding and is very suitable for work where a large number of similar joints, or where long runs, are needed. In spite of its limitations, it is probably more generally suited to use in the home workshop. There are no problems over safe storage of gases and one only has to pay for the electricity and welding electrodes as they are used.

When using arc welding equipment, do not work near combustible or inflammable materials like wood shavings or oil, or fires can be started. Normal electrical safety over fuses, earthing and care of cables must be attended to. The prime requirement, however, is to ensure that the user and any by-standers or assistants do not look at the arc without eye protection, even for a few seconds. Do not ever strike the arc unless eye protection is in place. The danger of the intense ultra-violet light given off by the arc cannot be overstressed. At best it can cause a temporary irritation known as arc-eye, at worst, permanent eye damage can result. This light can also cause 'sunburn' on exposed skin, so sleeves should be rolled down and the hand holding the electrode holder protected by a glove. Do not be put off by this: on balance, arc welding probably has fewer safety hazards associated with it than gas welding.

Spot Welding

This is another electric welding process that is widely used for joining thin sheet metal. It is often used instead of rivets, and as its name suggests, welds the metal together at one small area, or spot, commonly about 3mm (1/8") diameter. A large number of these spots are welded along the line of the joint, so holding the work together. Things like car bodies and metal office furniture are classic examples of the use of spot welding.

The method used is to clamp the work together between copper electrodes at the exact point of each weld. A powerful current is then switched on. As this passes through the work, the higher electrical resistance causes local heating, sufficient to melt the metal. The pressure from the electrodes unites the molten metal, which, when cool, holds the joint together. After one spot has been welded, the electrodes are moved apart, the work is moved along a little and the process repeated. In this way the whole joint is made by a series of spot welds spread out rather in the same way as a line of rivets.

Small spot welders are available that will work from a normal power point. They are rather expensive for the occasional job, and most people will probably not buy one for home use. If one is available (at an evening class, perhaps?) then it is a very useful, easy and quick way to join sheet metal.

Spot welding attachments are produced that connect onto small arc welding sets of the type sold for home use. These utilise a carbon electrode to locally heat the metal, which has to be held together by clamps and separately connected to the welding set for the return current. Touching the carbon electrode on the metal surface strikes an arc, the heat from which welds the metal at that point. From my somewhat limited use of one of these attachments, I can say that it works. It is, however, more time-consuming and does not produce quite such a neat job as a conventional spot welder. While using it, a normal arc welding face mask must be worn to protect the eyes.

Carbon Arc Torch
One of the disadvantages of an arc welding set, compared to gas welding equipment, is that it cannot be used for brazing. In an attempt to overcome this, carbon arc torches are produced. They consist of two carbon electrodes mounted in a holder with a handle. One electrode mount is free to slide towards or away from the other. Both electrodes are connected to the welding transformer, one to each terminal.

In use, the movable electrode is moved up to the fixed one until they touch and the moved slightly away. This starts up the arc, which is used in the same way as a flame to heat the work. It may be used for brazing, as intended, or for welding in the same way as an oxy-acetylene torch.

Brazing is often used on thin metal, especially steel, as a substitute for welding because the lower temperatures required reduce the risk of distortion. A carbon arc torch will do this work satisfactorily, but it is not the easiest way to go about it. The necessary arc welding

mask makes it less easy to see the work and the electrodes are slowly burnt away needing periodic readjustment to maintain the arc. This can be a nuisance on long seams. Given the choice, I would prefer to use oxy-acetylene or other gas equipment for brazing work, but if a welding transformer is the only item of equipment available, then a carbon arc torch will do the job.

Welding Procedure – General Comments
Whatever method of welding used, the edges of the metals to be joined must be prepared. This is sometimes no more than cleaning away dirt or truing up with a file. At other times, shaping, usually bevelling, is needed to help the welder to melt a sufficient depth of metal. This is usually required when working with thicker metal. Fig. 114 shows some typical joints and edge preparations used when welding, and Fig. 115 show the situation the welder must aim for when the joint is finished.

All welding, from a practical point of view, is a matter of practising until one has become sufficiently skilful to achieve the required effect. This is to melt the metal right through, without burning holes in it, and to melt a sufficient amount from the filler rod to fill the weld pool, in a continuous line, as long as the required weld. Obviously, this is not a skill that can be acquired

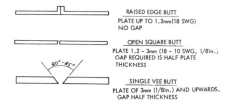

Fig. 114 *Edge preparation for welding.*

119

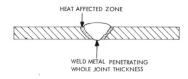

HEAT AFFECTED ZONE

WELD METAL PENETRATING
WHOLE JOINT THICKNESS

Fig. 115 *Cross-section of a weld.*

in a few minutes, or from simply reading descriptions. The important thing is to have the determination to keep practising until the techniques required are mastered.

Oxy-acetylene Welding

Start by opening the cylinder valves one quarter of a turn, no more is necessary, and check that sufficient gas is left in the cylinders. Fit the correct nozzle to the torch for the thickness of metal to be welded – this information is usually on the box containing the torch. If not, some experimentation is necessary.

Open one gas valve on the torch and turn the pressure regulator handle clockwise until the welding pressure gauge shows the correct pressure for the size of nozzle. Again, this information usually comes with the torch, but in the absence of any other advice, set to 5 lbs. per square inch and be prepared

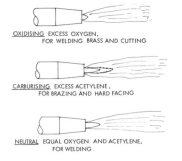

OXIDISING EXCESS OXYGEN.
FOR WELDING BRASS AND CUTTING

CARBURISING EXCESS ACETYLENE.
FOR BRAZING AND HARD FACING

NEUTRAL EQUAL OXYGEN AND ACETYLENE.
FOR WELDING.

Fig. 116 *Types of oxy-acetylene flame.*

to re-adjust later if necessary. Immediately this pressure is reached turn off the torch valve, then repeat for the other gas. It does not matter whether the oxygen or acetylene is dealt with first but the pressure must be set with the gas flowing.

To light the torch, open the acetylene valve a little, then use a spark type lighter or a match to light the gas, again while it is flowing. Open the acetylene valve further, until the flame just stops smoking, then open the oxygen valve until the welding flame (Fig. 116) is reached.

The metal should be prepared for welding and set up as already described. Play the torch flame around on the metal a little to pre-heat it, then direct the flame on the joint, moving it around in a small circle so that it heats both edges evenly. While doing this hold the filler rod, which must be made of the same metal as that being welded, so that its end is also heated by the flame. Aim to melt both edges and the end of the filler rod at the same moment. If this is correctly judged, the metal flows from the filler rod into the molten pool and fills it up. Once this stage is reached, move slowly along the joint a little and repeat the procedure. This should be done smoothly and evenly all the way along, each weld pool overlapping the previous one, until the end of the joint is reached. It should be one continuous joint, not a series of separate welds, and the metal should be melted right the way through. Fig. 117 illustrates this process.

Should the metal seem to be melting faster than it is possible to keep up with the filler rod, lift the torch away from the metal and continue again after it has cooled a little. If the problem continues check whether the nozzle is too large or

120

the gas pressure too high. The opposite could be the case if the metal seems reluctant to melt, or it could be that the torch is being held too far from the metal or moved along too fast. If the filler rod melts and not the work, it is most likely that the torch is being held at the wrong angle. These are some of the usual mistakes made by beginners, but, as already stated, the main thing is practice.

When welding is finished for a long period (overnight etc.), the cylinder valves should be turned off and the gas let out of the hoses and pressure regulators.

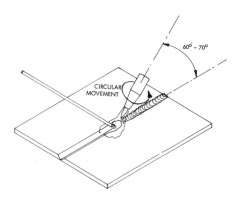

Fig. 117 *Gas welding in progress.*

Electric Arc Welding

In some ways this is easier to master than gas welding and it is certainly faster. Skill and practice are still, however, required to allow reliable, good quality work to be carried out, and the beginner should be prepared for some early failures and frustrations.

Fig. 118 illustrates the process, which starts by adjusting the welding transformer to provide the correct amperage for the metal and rods in use. Amperage settings are the equivalent of gas pressures in oxy-acetylene welding, but it is less easy to give hard and fast rules about them. One must be prepared to re-adjust if it seems there is too much or too little power. Usually, packets of welding electrodes and the transformer itself have information about current settings printed on them. In the absence of any more information or experience, set to the middle of the quoted range and work from there, re-adjusting as seems necessary.

After setting the welding current, assemble the work and clamp the return cable to it. This is frequently referred to as the earth, but it is not an earth

in the normal mains electricity sense. Make sure that there is no dirt or rust at the earthing point as a poor return current can prevent or spoil welding.

Select a suitable electrode. This must be made of the same metal as that being welded and must be a proper flux-coated one designed for arc welding. Ordinary gas welding filler rods will not work. Then grip the electrode in the holder by the short uncoated part at one end. Before switching on, make sure that the electrode and the holder are not touching any part of the work.

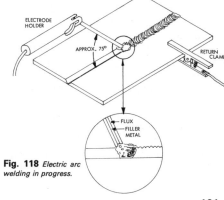

Fig. 118 *Electric arc welding in progress.*

121

Hold the electrode at an angle, just above the work at the point where welding is to start and put the face mask in place. Nothing can be seen at this point because of the thick ultra violet filter in the mask, so, by feel, the tip of the electrode is touched on the work. Bring the electrode up to a vertical position slowly so that the metal at the tip touches the work briefly then slope it again. This should start the arc, the light of which will allow the work to be seen and the electrode to be moved exactly into place. Welding is then a case of drawing the electrode slowly and evenly along the joint. Lifting it away from the work will break the circuit and stop the weld.

The most difficult part of the whole process is to get the arc started without the electrode sticking to the work. It requires some practice to get the feel of this stage and, even after this, difficulty may often be found in starting the arc. Dirt and rust on the surface of the work or the welding current set too low can prevent an arc being struck. This can also occur because the bare metal at the electrode tip is dirty or has a thin layer of flux over it. Holding it in contact with the work too long or having the current set too low can cause it to stick. If this happens, bend it backwards and forwards to break it off or, in an extreme case, unclip the holder and cut it off. If the arc does not seem to want to start even when all these conditions have been satisfied, scraping the end of the electrode along the surface of the work will usually succeed. Remember to keep the mask in place while doing all this.

When welding, proceed at the speed at which the electrode seems to want to go. If it is tilted, as in Fig. 118, the electrode holder can simply be moved nearer the work as the electrode melts

away and forms the joint. Try to avoid dragging it along the joint or holding it in one place for too long. The former will lead to a weak, uneven weld and the latter will melt holes in the work. Try to keep one corner of the flux coating resting on the work surface.

It would be possible to write many words of hints and tips this kind of welding. The main thing is to keep practising, trying to follow accurately the requirements until eventually the skill is acquired. Even after this, one should expect the odd 'off' day!

Distortion

This can be a problem in all welding work, but it is especially likely in thin sheet material. It is caused by the intense, but very local, heating setting up, or, ironically, removing stresses in the metal. Often it occurs during cooling as well as while welding is taking place.

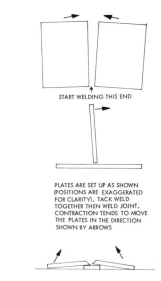

START WELDING THIS END

PLATES ARE SET UP AS SHOWN (POSITIONS ARE EXAGGERATED FOR CLARITY). TACK WELD TOGETHER THEN WELD JOINT. CONTRACTION TENDS TO MOVE THE PLATES IN THE DIRECTION SHOWN BY ARROWS

Fig. 119 *Minimising distortion when welding.*

Fig. 120 *Removing distortion by linear spot heating.*

Distortion usually takes the form of bending. bowing or rippling of sheets. It is more likely to occur on larger sheets than with smaller items.

Quite often it is satisfactory to ignore distortion until welding is finished and then press, hammer or mallet the work back into shape. Alternatively, set ups and working practices can be used to minimise or avoid it. These may be divided into three separate techniques.

The most easily applied method is to use weights, clamps, bolts, or a combination of all three, to hold the work exactly to shape. The general rule to follow is that any method used should be really firm and rigid. Some of the forces set in movement during welding are severe. Thick steel blocks can make useful flat surfaces to which work may be clamped, as can a steel bench surface, but leave a small air gap under the weld. Any clamps etc, should be left in place until the work is well cooled.

The arrangement of sections as they are set up before welding can be such that the distortion pulls them into the required alignment. Fig. 119 shows some standard examples of ways in which this is often done.

Heating is the third way of avoiding or removing distortion, and may be used before or after welding. Preheating can be used to generally heat the work. This relieves any cold working stresses present and minimise the effect of the localised welding heat. Care must be exercised over its use, however because it is possible to distort thin sheet simply by heating it generally. It is important to move the heat source around over the surface of the metal so that the whole surface is heated slowly and evenly, no one area being heated way beyond any other.

After welding, local heat may be used on the convex side of work to make it bend back into shape. This should be treated as a fairly precise process to the extent of chalk marking the areas to be heated. They should be brought to dull red only, as rapidly as possible, so that the heat does not spread too much. The width of the heated zone at the surface of the metal should be about one third of the length of the heated area. Fig. 120 shows an example of a situation in which this method may be used.

CHAPTER 9

Repair Work

Repair of sheet metal articles can become necessary because of corrosion, accidental damage or a combination of these factors. Because they can affect items in many different ways, it is not possible to describe every repair job that may come along. In this chapter, therefore, it is intended to describe some techniques which have been found useful and which, hopefully, may be adapted

Dealing with Rust Damage and Patching

Of all the corrosion types, rust is probably the best known and the one most frequently encountered. It only occurs in ferrous metals and is most common in mild steel. Other metals suffer from other forms of corrosion and the repair of areas damaged by this may be carried out using somewhat similar methods. Those mentioned here, however, are described with rust damaged areas particularly in mind.

An area pitted by rust, where the surface finish (usually, but not always, paint) has been lifted, can be coated with a proprietary rust treatment. There are many of these available in car accessory and decorating materials

shops. The surface being treated needs to be cleaned of loose rust, dirt and old paint and then treated according to the manufacturer's instructions. Repainting can follow. Chrome plated parts usually need cleaning and filing until all the rust has been removed and bright metal exposed. It is then possible to have them re-plated.

In more extreme cases, the rust affects the metal to the extent of making holes in it. Then, the affected area must be cut away, back to unaffected metal and patched in some way. There are various ways of doing this, depending upon the item.

If the item being repaired is made from fairly thick metal, then a good way of repairing a badly rusted area is to cut away the whole area affected back to good metal. A new piece of sheet is cut to fit and welded in place. The area cut away should not follow the irregular line of the rust but should be made to a convenient geometrical shape. Usually, a rectangle is most convenient when making the patch to fit into it. It can be given rounded corners if the possibility of stress cracks is thought likely. This method can be used with thinner steel items if it is important that the surface finish is retained. The welds can be filed or ground flat so that, after painting, the repair is barely detectable. Distortion, though, may prevent its use. If the rear surface is accessible the welding can be done from this side to reduce the amount of surface work needed.

Smoothing of welds on the surface is most easily accomplished using arbor-mounted grinding wheels or reinforced cutting discs held in portable power tools. The household electric drill will probably be used, but make sure goggles are worn to protect the eyes and that care is exercised in its use to avoid other injuries.

Where the outward appearance is less important than securing a repair, the rusted area may be cut away as before, or simply left as it is. Then a patch fixed over it on the surface will make the repair. On tinplate, thin steel items, and other metals that will take it, this can be soft soldered in place. It is useful in the repair of liquid containers like cans, buckets and such. Where thicker steel items are concerned, especially if strength is important, the patch may be welded on to the surface. Rust treatment and painting should always follow if the metal is steel.

If the patch does not need to be watertight, rivets may be used to hold it in place. Pop rivets are especially useful here as it may often be difficult to get rivet dollies behind the patch. This method is of use in many situations and will not damage surrounding paintwork or non-metallic trimmings. Although the patch will show, if the work is done neatly it need not be too unsightly, especially if countersunk rivets have been used.

Where the surface finish is important and welding is undesirable, the patch may be fixed behind the area being

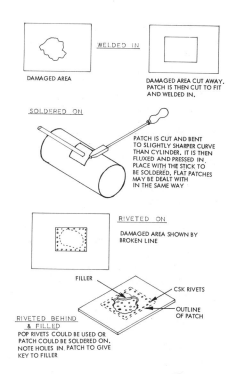

Fig. 121 *Patches.*

repaired. The resulting difference in surface levels can then be built up in some way. A further piece of sheet, of equal thickness to the original, may be cut to fit the hole and countersunk riveted to the patch. Filler around the edges of such a repair followed by filing and sanding can, with care, make it invisible after painting. Alternatively the whole surface could be built up with filler. If so, the patch should have a number of holes drilled in it to give a 'key'. The patch could be made of gauze or perforated sheet to save drilling.

Objections are sometimes raised to the use of filler but, properly used, it can

125

be quite successful. However, an alternative way to build up steel surfaces is the use of a material called body solder. This is used by professional car body repairers and may be spread over the heated surface by a wood block. It will not join direct to steel surfaces and these have to be tinned first with ordinary soft solder.

These methods are illustrated diagrammatically in Fig. 121.

Corroded Aluminium

The main problem in dealing with this metal is that it is difficult to solder and weld with the usual equipment available at home. In most respects other than this it may be dealt with as for steel, but without the use of soldering or welding. For a water-tight patch probably the easiest way is to use nuts and bolts or self-tapping screws to hold such patches in place. Self-tapping screws will be useful if only one surface is accessible. Before they are finally fixed the surface around the edges of the hole should be coated with mastic or jointing compound.

Repairing Dents

Repair methods used for dents rather depend on the size of the area affected. Small or shallow dents can often be pushed out by hand, especially if the metal is soft or they are in the centre of a large flat panel. Usually, however, dents need to be knocked out.

The simplest way to knock out dents is to use a mallet on the opposite side of the panel, and this is often effective. More than likely, however, the dent will have caused some stretching of the metal which prevents it from returning to its original shape. Methods akin to planishing then have to be used to stretch the surrounding areas and allow the dented area to be returned to its original shape.

If the whole panel can be removed from the item of which it is a part, then the work is made easier. The sheet can then be rested on a flat surface, or suitable stake, and the areas around the dent hammered so that they are stretched. If this is repeated at intervals between straightforward knocking out of the dent, eventually the original surface can be restored. Usually, as work proceeds, many local dimples and ripples are formed. These need planishing out individually until the surface is satisfactory. It is a time-consuming process requiring care and thoughtful work to achieve good results.

Things are more difficult if the dent must be knocked out while the panel is still in place. This is a common situation in motor car body repairs and only by using similar tools to the professional panel beater can a good looking repair be made. Typical panel beater's tools are shown in Fig. 122. They consist of long-necked hammers with slightly domed faces like planishing hammers and small hand-held anvils called dollies. The long necks on the hammers are to allow them to reach up inside deeply curved panels like wings. The dollies are usually made with a variety of curved and flat surfaces to fit the shape of the panels.

A dolly is selected to suit the shape of the panel concerned and is held behind a low spot. This is tapped from outside by a hammer to squeeze and stretch the metal, bringing it up to the level of the panel surface. Each low spot has to be worked out individually in this way. Panel beating is a time-consuming process and cannot be rushed. Light strokes with files of the type shown in Fig. 123 help to highlight the high spots so that the area requiring treatment can be seen.

For an occasional job it is possible to improvise panel beating tools. Small mild steel blocks, hard wood blocks, ball pein and planishing hammers may all be pressed into use to produce an acceptable result. This will never be quite as good as that which may be obtained with the proper tools and will need more effort with files, emery cloth and filler to work up a good surface.

If the back of the panel is not accessible and the dent not too severe it may sometimes be pulled out in the following way. Drill a small hole and partly screw in a self-tapping screw. Then use a carpenter's claw hammer on the screw to pull the dent out. The small hole left when the screw is removed can be filled and painted over.

Heat shrinking is a process that may be used to remove dents, but it requires care. A spot is selected to one side of the dent around 20mm (¾") diameter. This should be heated to red with an oxy-acetylene torch and the metal around it driven towards the centre by holding a dolly behind it and making light, rapid hammer blows. A number of such spots need treating around the dent to draw the metal in towards it. Finally planishing may be used to finish the surface.

On aluminium panels a lower temperature must be used. To judge this, soap can be rubbed on the surface and the heat only continued until the soap turns brown.

Quenching after heating with wet rags in this work can also help. This tends to shrink the metal and helps to pull it back into shape. Heat shrinking is not recommended until experience has been gained in the use of the heating equipment.

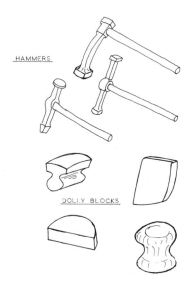

HAMMERS

DOLLY BLOCKS

Fig. 122 *Panel-beating tools.*

Removal of all but the shallowest dents requires a patient approach and a preparedness not to see results too quickly. Much work and effort is needed to restore the profile of curved panels and to produce a good surface on flat ones. Usually, the main part of the dent pushes or knocks out fairly easily. It is the effect of the stretching causing ripples and dimples over the affected area that takes time to correct.

Repairing Holes

Denting and accident damage can be so severe as to make holes in the metal. Holes resulting from accidental damage

Fig. 123 *Flexible body file.*

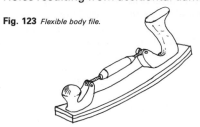

may be repaired using similar methods to those used for rust holes.

Where a hole is combined with denting, the dent should be dealt with first. Once the surface profile has been restored, the hole can be filled to match.

In home working, the best way to deal with small holes is to use a resin filler, perhaps reinforcing it with gauze or perforated sheet. Larger holes may be patched, but if the panel or section is curved, the patch will need curving to match. Any sort of curved repair is most easily made using filler, since it may be readily filed and sanded to shape. It will not do, of course, on items which are likely to get hot.

Using Resin Fillers

Resin fillers have been mentioned a number of times in this book, so some idea of their uses should already have been gained. They have many uses in sheet metalwork but are probably best known for their application to car body repairs. Many makes are available and they are easily obtained from garages and car accessory shops. It is not uncommon to find 'hard' and 'flexible' grades mentioned. The grade names describe the characteristics of the filler after it has set. 'Hard' grades will indeed be hard and brittle. They can be filed and sanded to give a very smooth surface which, after painting, is indistinguishable, visually, from a metal one. As an aside, painted-over filler repairs to steel items may be detected by using a magnet. 'Flexible' grade fillers are less hard and do not give quite such a good surface finish but they are more successful in absorbing small movements and vibration in the surrounding metal. They are more likely to 'stay put' under such conditions.

Fillers consist of a polyester resin mixed with a powder to give it body and a separate hardener. The resin/powder mixture has a small quantity of hardener added to it when ready for use. After thorough mixing, a spatula or filling knife is used to spread the filler, push it into corners and smooth the surface. Setting is brought about by chemical action between the resin and hardener, which varies according to temperature and make, but is typically between twenty and forty minutes. Often, the mixture gets quite warm when near the end of the setting period.

Manufacturers' instructions over mixing and use do vary slightly, so it is important to read and follow them carefully. Remember that the chemicals used, especially the hardener, are poisonous. Avoid skin contact and certainly do not let them get anywhere near faces, eyes, mouths or food.

The uses to which filler may be put are many and varied. Some have already been mentioned, but it sticks well to metal and may be used in many situations where small gaps and joints in metal items need to be made weather proof or simply disguised for cosmetic purposes.

When dealing with large areas, resin filler does not have sufficient strength on its own. Perforated sheet and gauze are sold to use as reinforcement. If used for car body repairs, or in other situations where water is likely to be present near a steel item, remember that they are often made from aluminium. This metal and steel rapidly corrode when they are together in the presence of water. Zinc or stainless steel gauze is produced and would be preferable, but it is not always easy to obtain. In this case, it would be better to reinforce the filler for a repair to a steel item with a piece of steel or galvanised steel sheet.

This should have a number of holes drilled in it to give a 'key' to the filler, which needs help to adhere to large surfaces.

An easy way of dealing with dents is simply to fill then up and sand smooth. Car and other vehicle bodywork may often be successfully repaired in this way, although some people may regard it as a 'bodge'. This is a pity because, used properly, it can allow someone inexperienced in panel beating and metalwork to effect an acceptable repair. The important thing is to drill the surface onto which the filler is to go. It can be forced into the holes to give a mechanical, as well as a chemical, bond between it and the metal surface. Fill to above the level of the surface then file and sand it to match. Any rust and corrosion should always be treated before using filler otherwise their effects will continue and eventually lift the filler or destroy the surrounding metal to which it is fixed.

Glass fibre work is sometimes confused with resin filler. The term is used to describe what should really be called glass reinforced polyester mouldings (G.R.P.). They consist of mouldings made up of resin and hardener without the filler powder but strengthened by a layer of glass fibre matting included in the moulding. Resin and hardener are mixed together and the resulting thick liquid is stippled onto the glass matting with a brush. Several layers may be built up on top of one another by repeating this process after the previous layer is set. In this way thicker and, therefore, stronger mouldings may be built up.

The production of G.R.P. mouldings is really a subject in its own right and the system is used to make many things where sheet metal or wood were once the only methods. Boat hulls, motor car

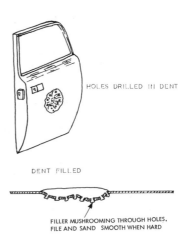

HOLES DRILLED IN DENT

DENT FILLED

FILLER MUSHROOMING THROUGH HOLES.
FILE AND SAND SMOOTH WHEN HARD

Fig. 124 *Repairing a dent with resin filler.*

bodies, and sections of railway locomotive and coach bodywork are frequently made in this way. I mention the system here as it does have some use in patching and repairing holes in sheet metal structures. Fig. 125 shows the general idea, but it must be pointed out that although this will give a satisfactory repair, it may well work out more expensive than using sheet metal. The advantages are that G.R.P. may be quicker and the repair can be made using simpler tools than those required for fixing metal patches.

Materials for making G.R.P. mould-

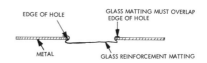

EDGE OF HOLE

GLASS MATTING MUST OVERLAP
EDGE OF HOLE

METAL

GLASS REINFORCEMENT MATTING

FIX GLASS MAT IN PLACE WITH SPOTS OF FILLER PASTE THEN BRUSH ON
RESIN/HARDENER MIXTURE. BUILD UP SURFACE WITH MORE LAYERS
OR WITH FILLER, THEN FILE AND SAND SMOOTH

Fig. 125

129

ings may be obtained from specialist suppliers who frequently advertise in the various hobby magazines. They may also be obtained over the counter in boat shops and yacht chandlers.

Repairs using filler and G.R.P. are very good in cosmetic and low strength situations. Car body work, water tanks, cans and buckets are situations where they may be found useful. They will not withstand much heat, however, and should not be used where this is likely to occur. Their advantage lies in the fact that they may be used away from power supplies and when only simple equipment is to hand.

Motor Car Body Repairs
Many of the techniques described in this chapter are applicable to the repair of motor car bodywork and that of other road vehicles. When dealing with modern cars, however, it is important to remember that they are often built without chassis. This means that many of the areas of the body are load bearing. If these places are damaged by corrosion or accident the method of repair, if repair is possible, should be such as to take this fact into account. Welding in or bolting on new sections are normally, for safety reasons, the only acceptable methods. Filler, G.R.P. and pop rivets should be kept for cosmetic repairs and not used on items like suspension mountings and sub-frames. Wings, door panels etc. are quite straightforward, but before making repairs to other areas it is wise to seek advice and to study the relevant workshop manuals.

CHAPTER 10

Spinning

Spinning is often used commercially for the production of hollow ware. It is of great advantage in repetition work, shaping the items produced more quickly than possible using the hand processes of raising or hollowing. Raised items are more easily made, the skill and patience involved in the hand process not being required. However, do not be misled by this as spinning requires skills of its own and is not as easy as we are sometimes told.

Vases, tea strainers, saucepans and many ornamental items are made from brass, copper, aluminium and its alloys, and stainless steel in this way. In amateur work, spinning can find a place in the production of dome covers for model steam locomotives, engine cowls for model aircraft and any similar round items. The process is especially useful when more than one item of identical shape is needed, the only major requirement being access to a suitable size lathe.

The principle of spinning is that a former and the blank are revolved together at high speed while the blank is forced by hand-held tool around the former.

Procedure

Fig. 126 shows a typical lathe set up for spinning. The former, which must be the same shape and internal size as the item to be spun, is held in the chuck. The blank, which is always a disc, is pressed firmly up against this with a pressure pad or mould, and very carefully adjusted to run true. This is important for the safety of both work and operator. Spinning may then be commenced by running the lathe at high speed and pressing the blank onto the former with the tool. Pressure for this is obtained by working the tool as a lever against a pin pushed into a suitable

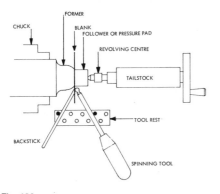

Fig. 126 *Lathe set up for spinning.*

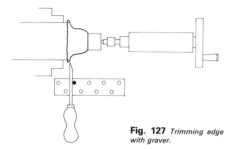

Fig. 127 *Trimming edge with graver.*

hole in the tool rest. Grease or thick oil should be applied to the end of the tool before, and at the intervals during, use. Start near the centre of the blank and work towards the outer edge.

During spinning, as with other sheet forming processes, the blank will become work-hardened very quickly. Frequent stops need to be made to re-anneal, and spinning, like other forming methods, has to proceed by easy stages.

When getting away from the central area, the hardwood back-stick is used to support the work behind the tool. This, and the tool, are then worked together, the back-stick holding the metal against the tool.

The tool should be used with a scooping type of action, gradually working towards the outer edge of the blank until the shaping is completed.

As more of the blank is shaped, the tool needs to be worked from a part of the rest nearer the former. The pins are moved to a hole nearer to it as necessary to permit this. Continue working towards the edge until the whole blank has been pressed down on to the former.

A wavy or irregular edge is often left and this may be removed with a hand held graver as in Fig. 127. An amount of metal to allow for this should be included in the diameter of the blank when it is first cut out.

The Lathe

Any lathe capable of running at high speed for reasonably long periods may be used for spinning, so long as the centre height is sufficient to accept the diameter of the blank. The lubrication system must be reliable and the cross slide or tool post capable of supporting the spinning tool rest. It is an advantage if the saddle can be clamped to the bed.

Certain items not found amongst the basic lathe equipment are needed, but these are of a kind that may be made without much difficulty by someone with a little experience of lathework.

Pressure Pad and Revolving Centre

Blanks may be held against the former in a number of ways. One way is to press them against it by means of a revolving pad held in the tailstock. The feedscrew is then used to apply the necessary pressure for the blank to be revolved by friction from the former.

The arbor holding this pressure pad should be fitted with a ball bearing to prevent friction. An example of a type suitable for construction by the home turner is shown in Fig. 128a.

A simpler arrangement, useful for occasional small jobs, is to make a separate pressure pad which may be held against the blank by an ordinary revolving centre. It would not be wise to attempt this with a plain tailstock centre as the friction caused by the lathe speed and the pressure would be very likely to burn it out. The arrangement is shown in Fig. 128b.

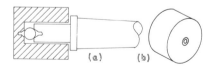

Fig. 128

Often the blank is held against the former by a cup shaped mould. This is a better arrangement but requires a separate mould for each different piece to be made. It does not, however, hold the work more securely than just relying on tailstock pressure.

These moulds are better held by a revolving centre but the normal type does not give as much support to the mould as possible. The type shown in Fig. 129 has a longer, thinner point than is usual, though it still needs to be of substantial thickness. This may be fitted into a deep hole drilled in the mould, giving better support than an ordinary centre locating in a shallow hole made with a combination drill.

The mould could be fitted with a ball bearing arrangement on the end of a Morse taper arbor, like the pressure pad, but this would make construction more difficult. Any number of different moulds may be used with one revolving centre.

Toolrest

This will have to be made to suit the type of lathe in use. It must be strongly made of thick material, preferably steel, and be able to be firmly fixed to the lathe. Often it is bolted on in place of the normal tool post. The design shown in Fig. 130 is intended to be bolted to the 'T' slotted cross slides that are found on many of the types of lathes in amateur use. In other types of machine a similar arrangement could possibly be used by removing the top slide and bolting it on

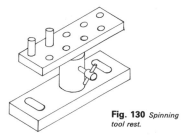

Fig. 130 *Spinning tool rest.*

in place of that, or it could be adapted to be held in the tool post.

Spinning tools should touch the work just below centre height and the height of the tool rest should take this into account. Its top surface requires a number of holes into which the fulcrum pegs must fit. These pegs and, therefore, the holes should be of sufficient diameter to withstand the leverage necessary. Four or five pegs should be made from round steel bar.

Tools

Most of the tools used for spinning are pressure tools, used to press the work around the former. A selection of such tools is shown in Fig. 131, together with the intended use of each. The ball-ended one may be regarded as a general purpose tool and will cope with a wide range of work.

Pressure tools must be strongly made from tool steel, their working tips must be made dead hard and their surfaces polished. If not, they will score and drag at the work surface, possibly tearing holes in it. They should be of a size compatible with the work to be undertaken, but long enough for there to be sufficient leverage to control them safely. Handles are best made of a close grained wood and should be at least 25mm (1″) thick and up to 500mm (20″) long, depending on tool and work size.

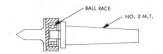

Fig. 129 *Thin revolving centre to hold spinning formers in place.*

133

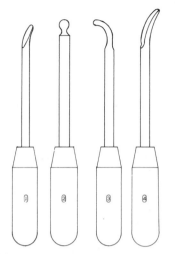

Fig. 131 *Spinning tools. 1, Smoothing. 2, Roughing and general purpose. 3, Recess forming. 4, Planishing or finishing tool.*

Old files can be softened and made into spinning tools, being hardened again after shaping.

After items have been spun, they are left with an irregular wavy edge. A graver is used to cut this off while the work is still set up in the lathe. Other methods may be used, but this is a quick, accurate and easy way. Gravers may also be made from old files and can find uses in other kinds of lathe work. They do not need to exert so much pressure as spinning tools and may, therefore, be a little more lightly made. As with all hand-held turning tools, however, they must be given strong smooth handles, long enough to permit sufficient leverage for them to be easily controlled.

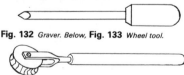

Fig. 132 *Graver. Below,* Fig. 133 *Wheel tool.*

Wheel tools are used to turn over edges to produce beads for strength and safety purposes. One is shown in Fig. 133.

Speeds
Generally speaking, lathe mandrel speeds for spinning should be fairly high. They need to be varied, as in other lathe work, to suit the type and size of metal in use, but also in thickness. The ideal speed for a particular job will need to be found by experiment, but as a guide, copper and brass may be run at approximately 1000rpm, aluminium a little faster and steel a little slower at around 700rpm.

Care is needed over speed because of the centrifugal forces set up. This requires especial care when thicker metal is in use, if it is not to be thrown out of the lathe. Lower speeds will be needed in this situation. Therefore, it is advisable to start at a slightly lower speed than ideal and to increase the speed cautiously until the best combination of ease of work and safety are found. Lathes with infinitely variable speed control are an asset in this sort of situation.

Safety
Apart from the normal dangers present when using a lathe, spinning has a number of others against which precautions need to be taken. Most of these dangers concern the fact that a large metal disc with fairly sharp edges is being revolved at high speed while held in place by little more than friction.

Apart from commonsense precautions like keeping hands out of the way of the spinning blank, it is most important to make sure that sufficient pressure is being exerted by the tailstock to hold it in place. It is also important to make sure that the blank is set up so that it will run true. Dial gauge accuracy may not be required, but it is certainly necessary to take the time to see that it is running visually true. If not, it is quite likely to be thrown out sideways once the lathe is running.

Because of the nature of the spinning operation, it is also a good idea to wear leather gloves while operating pressure tools, certainly during the early stages. When working with hand-held tools of this kind it is all too easy to slip, especially if one is inexperienced in their use. The danger of this is that the hands could land with some force against the outer edge of the blank.

To avoid the risk of injury when using pressure tools, it is important to make sure that the tool rest and fulcrum pegs are securely fixed in place. Make sure bolts are firmly but not over tightened and if the rest is a type that is held in the lathe tool post make sure that is firmly fixed in place. The compound, or top slide, may also pivot under pressure, so it is wise to check the clamping screws or bolts for that. Handles of tools should be repaired or replaced if loose or split.

If things should go wrong, protective clothing, especially a face shield, but also a leather apron, will help prevent serious injury. So too will developing the habit of standing away from a direct line with the work. If it should fly out you can then watch it whiz past your ear with a certain amount of detachment.

Finally, exercise caution over use of speed. Spinning is a process that needs to be carried out at high speed, but be under rather than over enthusiastic in the use of this. It is better to set the speed a little low than risk having metal discs flying about the workshop.

Formers

For light duty work these can be made from hard wood. Brass and mild steel may also be used, with mild steel being necessary if a former is to receive a great deal of use.

The shape of a former must match the shape to be produced and sometimes more than one former will be required if a shape needs to be produced in more than one stage. Dimensionally, the former must, of course, fit the inside of the item. It is easy to forget this point.

The simplest formers may be made from one piece of material turned to size in the lathe. Small ones may be held in a chuck whilst larger ones will need to be screwed or bolted to the face plate. Fig. 134 shows a former that could be used for an engine cowl for a model aircraft. The centre hole in the cowl would need to be cut after spinning.

A better arrangement is when a sec-

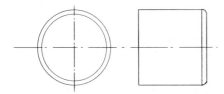

Fig. 134 *Spinning former for engine cowl.*

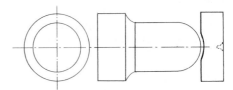

Fig. 135 *Spinning former for steam dome.*

(No dimensions given as drawings are intended as a general guide to shapes possible.)

135

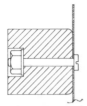

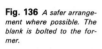

Fig. 136 *A safer arrangement where possible. The blank is bolted to the former.*

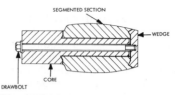

Fig. 137 *Collapsible spinning former.*

ond part is added to the former, called a mould. This may be made in the same way, and from the same materials as ordinary formers, but because it fits around a part of the work and helps to hold it in place it is safer. It is a better method when deep items need to be spun since these will require larger discs which take more holding. A former and mould suitable for making a dome cover for a model steam locomotive are shown in Fig. 135.

When the workpiece may be permitted to have a small hole in its centre, this may be used to fix it to the former with a screw. This method is to be preferred whenever it is possible to use it, because it gives a reliable and positive way of holding the blank to the former. The need for a mould or pressure pad is also removed. Either the dome cover or the engine cowl could be produced in this way and a sketch of the kind of set up involved appears in Fig. 136.

Quite often items need to be produced with necks narrower than their bodies. The difficulty here is that a normal former could not be removed from the spinning after shaping was complete. In a situation like this a collapsible former is used. This is made in sections which are securely held together during spinning but which may be separated for removal afterwards. A mould of this kind is shown in Fig. 137. It is best made from mild steel or brass, but hard wood could be pressed into service. First a

solid block should be roughed out to the approximate shape by turning, leaving it well over-size. This is sawn into the various sections and the sawn surfaces filed smooth. The pieces are then soft soldered back together. After finish turning to shape, the sections may be separated by heating and the mating surfaces cleaned up. In use, they are held together by the wedge and its fixing screw tapped into the outer end of the former. Removing this screw, when spinning is complete, allows the former to be dismantled and its pieces removed from the spun shape.

Metals Available for Use

Thin copper, brass, aluminium alloy, stainless and mild steel are frequently shaped by spinning. For amateur and home use it is probably best to keep to the softer and more ductile ones, avoiding the steels.

Metal up to about 1.5mm (16swg) thick may be hand spun using the methods described here, but working with metal below this thickness will be found easier from the point of view of the physical effort required. Very thin metal is much easier to tear and form corrugations in during spinning and if working with anything below 0.5mm (25swg) this may cause problems.

For anyone trying out spinning for the first time, it is probably best to make something of fairly, but not very, small diameter from copper or aluminium alloy about 1mm (20swg) thick.

CHAPTER 11

Finishing Processes

Finishing processes are used after construction to protect or improve the appearance of the workpiece. The type of finish employed will depend upon the use to which the item will be put and the environment in which it will be used.

So many materials and methods are available for finishing metalwork that it is not possible to go into great detail or to describe all of the possibilities here. It is hoped, however, that the information given in this chapter will allow suitable finishing methods to be selected for normal home sheet metalwork.

Preventing Rust and Corrosion
While most metals will corrode, given suitable conditions, in normal use none do so as quickly as mild steel. Therefore, it is with this metal that most of our corrosion prevention needs to be concerned. Stainless steel and most non-ferrous metals are much more resistant to corrosion and are frequently left untreated, except, perhaps, for polishing. Many methods are used to prevent rust, by far the most common form of corrosion, of mild steel. The method selected must take into account the use to which the item will be put, the length of time protection is needed and the severity with which the steel is likely to be attacked.

Rust is caused by moisture, chemicals and oxygen attacking the surface of the steel. Anything which will prevent any of these touching the surface will stop rust. If any of the coating is removed, even if a pin hole occurs in it, then rusting can start at that point and spread underneath the protective coating. This can lift the coating causing further attack and so a sort of chain reaction begins. Water, chemicals ageing and accidental knocks can all damage the protective coatings used on steel and they should be chosen so that their durability matches the most likely kinds of attack.

Oil
This is a good rust preventer, but it is comparatively easily removed by any sort of rubbing or washing action. The heavier the oil, the less easily it is removed, but oiling should only be regarded as a temporary way to stop rust. It is a useful method of stopping rust forming on steel items while they are under construction during the intervals between work periods. It is also a good way to protect steel tools while they are out of use.

Rusty areas awaiting treatment may be coated with oil to stop any further rusting before they can be dealt with.

Any oil will protect against rust, but the thicker oils will 'stay put' better, while thinner ones will penetrate crevices better. Dirty engine oil is quite good for rust protection and does not cost anything. Spray-on penetrating oil, available in aerosols, is a very convenient way of quickly coating an object.

Apart from lubrication, oil is very good at preventing rust on moving parts. These are not so frequently encountered in sheet metalwork as in other types, but hinges, for example, are often made from sheet metal. They may be painted but this will soon wear off the pivot pin and the rubbing faces. A little attention to these from time to time with the oil can, especially if they are used outdoors, will stop them rusting and prevent squeaky or stiff operation.

Grease

Like oil, grease is useful for the protection of otherwise untreated surfaces, but is less easily removed. It is good for protecting stored metal until it is ready for use. If grease is softened by warming it may be applied by brush. Removal can be effected with paraffin, by warming the component then wiping it off or by using a degreasing agent, such as Gunk.

Blueing in Oil

This is a very good means of preventing rust on polished steel surfaces when the item concerned is not going to be used in a hostile environment. It will not protect, for very long, items left permanently out of doors, but it is very good for tools, templates and other items usually kept under moderately favourable conditions. The easiest items to treat are those of relatively small size, although it is quite feasible to blue larger components. It simply requires more time and care.

Articles being blued are polished with emery cloth and gently heated until the oxide which forms on the surface turns to a blue or blue-black colour. For the best appearance, colouring needs to be even over the whole surface and this may only be achieved if care is taken over the heating. When the blue stage is reached, the item is cooled by quenching in a tin of oil. After cooling, it is removed from the oil and wiped dry. The result is an oil-impregnated film of oxide over the surface of the steel which may range from a mid-blue to a black colour, depending on the length of time it was heated.

The best oil to use for blueing is dirty engine oil, although other types can be used.

For heating, a gentle flame may be used with the object being treated held with tongs or on a length of wire. It is moved about slowly in the flame, judging the progress by the oxide colours as they form.

A better heating method is to use a sand tray. This is a shallow metal tray, of a size to suit the work anticipated, full of dry sand. It is rested over a gas ring and the item being heated laid in it. The sand diffuses the heat, helping to spread it more evenly over the item.

When blueing in this way, it is important not to allow the work to reach red heat, even a dull red. It is possible to set fire to the oil if red hot metal is placed in it.

At the start of quenching, the oil smokes for a short time. This smoke should be kept away from naked flames as it is fairly inflammable. Also, and especially if a lot of blueing work is being done, it is wise to ensure good ventilation in the working area to clear the smoke. A nearby door or window left open is usually sufficient.

While not very great, if normal care is taken, there is a fire risk attached to this process. For this reason, it is a good idea to have a fire blanket, or some other smothering device, available. If the oil does catch fire, it is soon put out if a folded up fire blanket is placed firmly over the top of the tin.

Painting

The use of paint is by far the most common and best known finish used on metals. It protects against rust or corrosion and is one of the most versatile and easily applied methods of decoration.

There are many kinds of paint available today but all have certain things in common. The most important of these is the need for correct preparation of the surface before painting starts.

All paints form a film over the surface of the metal to which they adhere and protect it against corrosive attack. Anything which will stop this film being formed or adhering must be removed before painting starts. Dirt, oil, grease, rust and water must be thoroughly and carefully removed.

With certain exceptions, bare metal surfaces should always be coated with a suitable primer before undercoat and top coat are applied. The primer adheres to the metal more reliably than other paints and helps to hold the later coats in place. Some primers contain rust or corrosion inhibiting chemicals, and others are designed for use over rusty areas, once any loose rust has been removed. It is important to choose

the right type for the metal being painted and to make sure it is compatible with the finishing paint to be used. The main rule here is to avoid using cellulose based paint over oil based primer.

Tinplate may be painted without using primer if a quick job is needed. For the best work, however, it should be primed.

If a surface has been painted at an earlier date and needs repainting, it is usually only necessary to clean and rub down the old paint before re-painting. Bare metal, and rusty areas where the old paint has fallen off, should be treated and primed as for new metal.

For maximum protection, of both the metal and the paint finish, a coat of varnish is a good idea. This is especially useful where the paintwork includes decorative lining, signwriting and so forth. Maintenance is then a matter of rubbing down and re-varnishing at intervals.

Individual types of paint will be considered in more detail later on. It is relevant here, however, to point out that oil based paints seem, from observation, to be more effective at preventing rust than cellulose based ones.

Rust-proofing Waxes

Several makes of these have come on to the market during the last ten years or so. They are intended to be used for rust-proofing the under surfaces of motor car bodies but may be used on any steel item that needs protection from water and salt attack. Car accessory shops and suppliers often sell them and others are advertised in newspapers and magazines as being available on mail order.

After application these rust treatments dry to a soft waxy texture which never completely hardens. Any small chips or scratches tend to fill up again as the wax spreads into them. They are, therefore, very resistant to having the protective film permanently punctured.

As supplied, these rust treatments are in the form of a liquid and may be applied by brush or spray. Using a syringe (often supplied by the manufacturers) and a length of tube, they may be applied to the inside of box sections.

Bare metal can be protected by these products, but it is probably better if they are used over paint. I say this because the places in which they are intended to be used have usually been painted first and so one assumes that this gives a 'belt and braces' situation of maximum possible protection. Some of them are advertised as being able to stop rust after it has started, as well as preventing it starting.

Since they remain soft these rust treatments tend to attract dust and dirt, so they are not really for use in situations where appearance is of importance. Where this is unimportant or secondary to protection, then these wax type treatments could well be of use. They give a long lasting and very effective protection against rust and chemical attack from salts, and could be used on tanks, pipes and gutters as well as motor cars.

Combinations of Metals that may Cause Corrosion

When two different metals are immersed in an electrolyte they can begin to work like a battery. This is called an electrolytic cell and the electricity is formed chemically by one metal being attacked at the expense of the other.

Electrolytes are electrically conductive liquids and things like sea water, salt road spray in winter and acid rain are every day examples.

It may be seen, therefore, that articles made of two or more metals are likely to have at least one of the metals rapidly corroded when in the presence of these liquids. Even pure water is reported as having a slight effect.

Fig. 138 lists some of the common metals in the order of what is known as the electro-chemical series. This lists metals in order of their voltage potential when in the presence of an electrolyte and give some guidance to their relative abilities to resist corrosion. The further apart any two metals are, the greater is the possibility of corrosion, with the lower metal being attacked in favour of the higher one. Metals close to each other may both be attacked.

A metal's position in this list is partly dependent on the electrolyte used and variations of position and value can occur with different liquids. As a further guide, Fig. 138 also lists the various metals with respect to their behaviour in sea water.

This information may be used to help prevent corrosion in a number of ways, although it should not be regarded as the whole answer.

At the planning stage of a job, metals can be selected that are less likely to corrode in the conditions of service envisaged, so long as they comply with any other requirements.

If undesirable combinations of metals must be used, it is sometimes possible to ensure that they are electrically insulated from each other. This can be done by inserting a thin plastic membrane or forcing mastic between them. If this is not possible, then an effort must be made to prevent the metals

FIG. 138

ELECTRO-CHEMICAL SERIES TABLE

METAL	POTENTIAL
Silver	+ 0.80
Copper	+ 0.35
Lead	− 0.13
Tin	− 0.14
Nickel	− 0.25
Cadmium	− 0.42
Iron	− 0.44
Zinc	− 0.77
Aluminium	− 1.34

POTENTIALS IN SEA WATER

METAL	POTENTIAL
Zinc	− 1.10
Galvanised Iron	− 1.05
Aluminium	− 0.75
Mild Steel	− 0.70
Lead	− 0.55
Tin	− 0.45
Brass	− 0.26
Monel	− 0.20
Stainless Steel	− 0.05 to 0.20
Nickel	− 0.15
Silver	0.00

coming into contact with moisture. Painting and plastic coating are ways in which this may be done.

Corrosion may be prevented by the use of sacrificial anodes. In any combination of metals, the one with the lowest voltage potential is called the anode. As already seen this corrodes in favour of the other metal, which is called the cathode. If a metal that is very anodic to the one needing protection is selected, a block of it may be fixed to, or near, the object concerned and connected electrically to it. This will then corrode, and, in doing so, give protection to the boat, fence, tank or whatever.

Sacrifical anodes are usually made of zinc because this has a lower potential than most other metals. At intervals they must be replaced before they are entirely corroded or there will be a loss of protection.

Paints
Of all the surface finishes available, paint is probably the most generally useful and the easiest to apply. It may be used with only the simplest of tools and is both protective and decorative. Its only real disadvantage is that painted articles need re-coating from time to time, the frequency with which this is necessary depending upon where and how the item is used.

Most metals may be painted but some do not need it for protection and it is often customary to leave these unpainted. Copper, brass, aluminium, lead and zinc are often treated in this way, being quite corrosion resistant, even if permanently exposed to the weather. Sometimes they are painted, however, if they need to match other parts or to be a definite colour, aluminium alloy panels on motor vehicle bodies and brass bodywork on model locomotives being examples of this.

Paint chemistry is a wide and complicated subject and there is a bewildering variety of paints on the market. Here, the aim is to consider the main kinds available for metalworking use, together with their advantages and disadvantages.

Surface Preparation
Assuming a new item that has not been painted before, the first step is to remove oil, grease, dirt and all traces of soldering flux.

Often a wipe over with a rag is sufficient for oil and grease, but it is better to be more thorough than this. There are several de-greasants on the market and these can usually be spread over the surface and worked into corners and crevices with a brush. An old toothbrush is ideal. Following this, the workpiece is washed well in running water to remove the degreasant along with the oil and grease which it has dissolved.

Soft soldering fluxes can usually be removed by running water. If they are more stubborn, as paste fluxes can sometimes be, warm water into which some detergent or washing up liquid has been added will usually work.

Hard soldering fluxes are not so easy since they usually leave a hard glaze which is resistant to files and scrapers. Pickling in dilute sulphuric acid is often successful in loosening them sufficiently for them to be filed or scraped away. This cannot be used with steel items and then it is a case of laborious chipping and scraping away until all traces are removed. Scrapers made from pieces of old hacksaw blades can be useful here.

Brazing fluxes seem to have the hardest surface after cooling and can take the edges off files and chisels. Apart from pickling, which can help, and the use of small mounted grinding wheels there is no other way than to patiently chip and scrape them away by hand. It is important they are removed, however, because they will surely flake away at a later date, taking any overlying coats of paint with them.

Solder lumps and any other heavy blemishes can be removed with files and scrapers to give a smooth surface. Bumps and irregularities are highlighted by gloss paint and varnish.

Light dirt and any surface rust can be removed with emery cloth, of a medium to fine grade. This material is also good for the final surface treatment before painting commences. The ideal surface should be clean and smooth without being polished. Light emery cloth scratches give a good 'key' to the paint, as do those left by a wire brush. A polished surface is not recommended.

Primer

Bare metal should, normally, be primed before using finishing paints. The primer used should be compatible with the solvents used in the paint to follow it.

Chromate primers are good for use on a variety of metals, although they are at their best on iron and steel. They are good when the item has to weather well and where there is some rust present.

Red oxide primers also work well on steel and may be obtained in cellulose or oil based forms as well as in the form of aerosols. They can be used with all metals.

Paints sold just as 'metal primer' tend not to be so protective as other types. They will certainly work, but are best for use in less arduous situations.

Self-etch primers are the best to use on aluminium, brass, zinc or galvanised steel. These metals tend not to take paint so well and self-etch primers, which chemically etch themselves into the surface while drying, give a better bond. They are usually cellulose based, may be coloured or clear, and can be overpainted with either oil or cellulose based paints.

Primer should not be rubbed down, or only very lightly. Over-enthusiastic rubbing down can scrape away the paint in places, which means that the next coat will be going on to bare metal at that point.

Oil Based Paints

These are the traditional types of paints. House paints, modelling enamels, primers and many others are oil based. They may be brushed or sprayed, but are not widely available in the form of aerosols. Almost any painting work can be done with oil based paints and they can be rightly regarded as the general purpose variety.

For outdoor use they are more durable than other types with regard to weathering and may correctly be used for protecting and decorating outdoor steelwork.

Like most paints the finishing or gloss coats are best applied over an undercoat although some of the modern ones are designed to be used without this. Several thin coats are preferable to a thick one and work should be rubbed down between coats with silicone carbide paper. If used wet this will give a smoother surface, and, therefore, a better finish to the next coat.

As a general rule, oil paints are best when a high gloss finish is wanted without further attention such as polishing. They also flow better than other types and are, therefore, better for lining and signwriting.

Cellulose Based Paints

These paints have a harder surface finish than oil based paints but are not so resistant to weathering. They may be obtained in ordinary tins suitable for brush applications, but are most frequently sprayed. Car touch-up aerosols usually contain cellulose based paints, although modern new cars are not usually painted with them. Oil based paints are used for this, but because of their formulation and the fact that they are hardened by baking, it is possible to paint over them using cellulose, with no ill effect.

Normally, cellulose paint must not be used over oil paint because the solvents used in the cellulose will cause the oil paint to ripple and lift. Barrier paints can be obtained which can be painted over oil-based paint to protect it if it must be covered by cellulose.

Cellulose paints are able to be polished to give a shinier surface, and this is necessary to achieve the best finish when using them. Metal polish or a cutting paste with a power-driven lambswool mop are usually used for this, although hand methods can be employed. This gives a much better finish than is possible with oil based paints and, being harder, it is less likely to be damaged by accidental knocks. Their weathering ability, however, is less good than oil paint.

Polyurethane Paints

These are oil base paints that are chemically modified. Their principal feature is that they dry with a harder surface than ordinary oil paints without the unpleasant fumes associated with cellulose paints. Some are manufactured in the form of jelly type non-drip paints which are often advertised as needing no undercoat.

These paints may be used perfectly well on metal with the same technique as ordinary oil paints. They do not seem able to give such a glossy finish and are less durable when subjected to attacks by the weather. I would consider them to be of most use for giving a quick cosmetic finish to items that will be principally used, or stored, indoors. With their harder surface they could be of use on toys.

Specialised Paints

There are many of these and it is worth investigating the types available if one wants to obtain maximum protection or more striking appearances. Those which I consider to be of most use for the sort of work described in this book are briefly considered in the following paragraphs.

Bituminous paint is an oil based paint which is black. It is fairly soft and is not very resistant to lubricating and other oils. Its main attributes are that it is able to give a very thick and water resistant coating and will fill up minor gaps and pin-holes if applied thickly. A primer is needed but no undercoat. The main purpose of this paint is the protection of steelwork from attack by water.

Zinc coating paints are also intended to protect steelwork against rust and corrosion. Being anodic to steel, the zinc will continue to help protect it even if the paint receives small scratches. These paints are usually considered to be primers and although they may be left as applied, they are best when covered by a coat of finishing paint.

Heat resistant paints are sold in motor car accessory shops for painting engines. They can be used anywhere that is likely to get hot, such as smoke-box and boiler cladding on model steam locomotives.

Metallic finish paints are acrylic based and contain small flakes of metal which give them a very striking finish. They are popular on motor cars, especially in aerosol form and are a good way to give something a more striking and unusual finish. Care is needed in their use if the best finish is to be obtained, and obtaining a good match when touching up damaged paintwork can be difficult.

'Hammerite' is the trade name given to a range of paints which dry to give a mottled surface effect known as hammer finish. They offer a good way of obtaining an unusual surface texture which many people find quite attractive, but have some other, very useful, characteristics. Not least of these are the facts that no primer or undercoat is required and that excellent rust protection is given to ferrous metals, even if they were already rusty when painted. Often only one coat is required. These paints are, therefore, extremely useful when a quick and protective paint job is required. From my own use of them they certainly seem to live up to their manufacturer's claims. On the debit side, they are not so easy to obtain as other paints, often having to be obtained by mail order. Whiston's of Stockport keep them (mail order or callers), and they can also often be found in boat and car accessory shops. There is a more limited range of colours available than with other paints and they do not give a high gloss finish, but this is a small price to pay for their other qualities.

Varnish

When maximum life is needed from a paint finish or when lining, signwriting and transfers have been used it is a good idea to protect it all with a coat of varnish. The finishing coat and any painted lining and lettering are very lightly rubbed down with fine grade silicon carbide ('wet-or-dry') paper. Then any transfers are applied, followed by the coat of varnish. Several coats of varnish may be applied over the years to restore the surface if it becomes dull before a complete re-paint is needed.

There are, basically, two sorts of varnish available for use in this kind of work, polyurethane and ordinary oil based varieties. Their characteristics are much the same as those possessed by oil and polyurethane paints and they should be used in similar situations. Various useful varnishes and transfer fixatives are available in aerosol form, usually from artist's suppliers and model shops.

Lacquers
These are high quality, quick drying varnishes, often cellulose based, that are intended for giving clear and coloured finishes to jewellery and other decorative work. They also find use on cameras and other photographic equipment, some being available that produce a dead matt black finish that reflects no light.

Clear lacquers will probably be of most use for the sort of work described in this book. They may be used on polished surfaces to prevent tarnishing or oxidizing by the atmosphere.

Lacquers may be brushed or sprayed and small items can be dipped. Dipping is quite simple to do. The item concerned is hooked onto a piece of bent wire to provide a handle and some lacquer is poured into a small tin. Just enough lacquer should be used to cover the item concerned which is lowered into the lacquer until it is completely submerged. It is then lifted out and allowed to drip until one 'tear' remains that seems reluctant to fall off. A piece of absorbent cloth is just touched against this without touching the metal. The item is then hung up out of the way of any dust until the lacquer is dry. Usually this is only a matter of a few minutes.

Many people do not like a lacquered finish because it can change the appearance of the polished metal slightly. The best ones, correctly used, can be virtually undetectable when new, but can yellow with age if exposed to heat or strong light. Even yellowed lacquer looks better than tarnished brass or copper work, though, and if something is going to be difficult to keep polished it is a good idea to lacquer it. The appearance aspect is largely a matter of personal feelings.

Plastic Coating
Metal items can be coated with a layer of plastic to decorate and protect them. The method is frequently used with steel items but other metals may be coated as well. It is a good method to use in situations where paint might be quickly scratched and where the surface is rather rough for good appearance.

Small articles may be coated at home if the powder can be obtained. They are heated in the domestic oven until they are nice and hot, too hot to hold in the hand. Then they are laid in the plastic powder, which should be tipped into a shallow tray, and moved around so that a good layer of powder is sticking to the areas required. The article is then put back in the oven for a few minutes, until the coating of plastic has smoothed over, and then taken out and left to cool. Any surplus coating can be cut away with a knife, and it is a good idea to lay a steel sheet in the bottom of the oven to catch any drips, although these could be peeled away when cool. Soft soldered items should not be plastic coated.

Plastic coating is frequently used commercially and firms who do this work will often do individual jobs. This is a useful service when items of a large size are involved or when it is felt not to be worthwhile using the process at home.

Plating
Plating is where a metal's surface is coated with another metal which is deposited electrically. It is used for protection, decoration or both, and many

combinations are possible. Information on the practical side of the subject for the home worker has been published, but unless one is very interested in it as a process, electro-plating is best left to specialists. The Yellow Pages telephone directory usually lists electro-platers and they will often deal with individual items.

Chromium plating will both protect and decorate. It is normally used on brass and steel and gives a hard, attractive and corrosion-resistant surface. When used on steel it can encourage rusting if any of the coating has pin holes or is damaged, but it is otherwise very protective.

Zinc plating gives a protective coating on steel, and is known as galvanising. It is very effective, long lasting and discourages rusting, even if the coating becomes damaged. Galvanising is very good in arduous situations.

Nickel is often plated on to steel articles to give protection and decoration. It is less shiny than chrome but is often found to be more attractive for this reason.

Silver plating is a good way to finish decorative work in brass or gilding metal. It gives the appearance of a silver article without the expense of making it from the solid metal. Silver plated articles are best lacquered to prevent tarnishing because repeated polishing can wear away the plated coating, which is comparatively thin.

Anodising

The surface of aluminium and its alloys may be oxidised electrically to give a coating that will prevent further oxidation and, therefore, corrosion. Anodised surfaces are naturally grey but other colours, such as blue, red and gold, can be put into the oxide film to serve as a means of decoration. It is a very effective way of protecting the aluminium, and anodised articles need no other treatment, even in quite severe environments as found on boats.

Polishing

All the metals in everyday use can be polished, but some respond better than others. Non-ferrous metals tend to polish better than ferrous ones, but stainless steel is an exception to this rule. Copper, brass and silver are the most usual metals to be finished by polishing.

Polishing means reducing the scratches on the surface of a piece of metal until they are too small to be seen by the naked eye. It is a simple but laborious process and much time and effort is required to work up a good polished finish on a piece of metalwork.

If a piece of work is to be given a polished finish, the fact should be borne in mind from the earliest stages of construction. Care should be taken not to unnecessarily scratch the surface when marking out, filing or holding in the vice. Work of this sort is often best held in a piece of folded cartridge paper when gripped by the vice and when stored between working sessions.

Apart from these points, polishing normally has to be the last stage of construction. All flux and oxide must be removed and the surface carefully examined for scratches. Deep ones can be gently filed to remove them using a smooth cut file. Filed areas then need draw filing, holding the file by its blade and working it from side to side instead of forwards and backwards. This produces a smoother surface than normal, or cross, filing.

The next stage is to use emery cloth, if possible wrapped around a file blade or small piece of wood. Start with a medium grade and work over the whole surface with it until no file scratches are visible when it is closely examined. Then go to a finer grade of emery cloth and work over the surface with it until the scratches from the previous grade are no longer visible. Work down to the finest (smoothest) grade of emery cloth you have available in stages like this. Silicon carbide paper can be used for an even better finish as this is produced with smaller grits than emery cloth.

Once the best finish possible with emery cloth has been attained final polishing may be started. The normal way this is done is to hold the metal against the edge of a mop made of discs of linen which is revolved at high speed. Polish, known as buffing compound, is rubbed on the surface of the mop. This is a mild abrasive and works the surface of the metal up to a shine. Different grades of buffing compound are available to produce general purpose or finer finishes and for different types of metal. It is possible to work up to an extremely good finish in this way.

Buffing or polishing machines are very much like bench grinders with the guards removed and the grinding wheels replaced by polishing mops. To adapt a grinder for this use a tapered spindle nose is needed. This threads on the spindle of the grinder and then fits into the leather washer in the centre of the polishing mop. When using such a machine, keep loose clothing out of the way and remember to hold work on the lower part of the wheel, below its centre line. If it should get caught up on the wheel it will not then be thrown out at you, but will go on to the floor. Also, remember that buffing can generate a lot of heat and it is often advisable to wear leather gloves to avoid burning the hands.

If no polishing machine is available, work may be clamped to the bench and polished with a small mop, or a lambswool bonnet held on an arbor in a hand held electric drill. Normal buffing compound may be used or a liquid metal polish, such as 'Brasso', but this is milder than the buffing compound and will take longer.

To polish inside articles, specially shaped mops are needed. Standard ones can be bought, but it is often a case of making them up from wood dowel and felt to suit the work in hand.

When the insides of small handles and other features with holes in them have to be polished it is sometimes necessary to use string coated with buffing compound or jeweller's rouge. Avoid this whenever possible as it is most laborious, but sometimes it is the only way.

Polishing is hard work but it is very rewarding to see an item on which much care and work has been lavished gradually acquiring a beautiful deep shine. Brass and copper are especially attractive when polished and small details made from them can have a great cosmetic effect upon items made mainly from other materials. Their appearance when polished is one characteristic which lifts metals above many other materials from an appearance point of view.

Sheet Thickness

In the text, the nearest standard thickness of metric sheet to the swg size has been quoted. The figures given here are more accurate equivalents, so there will be minor discrepancies between the two. Remember metric sheet metal is not available in these exact thicknesses, but in rounded off ones that are roughly equivalent.

For practical purposes, therefore, 1mm sheet can be used in place of 18swg, 1.5mm in place of 16swg and so on.

If thickness is critical, such as in boiler making work, it is best to use the nearest metric size sheet above the swg equivalent. This way, safety margins will not be decreased. For example, if the drawing specified 12swg copper sheet and only metric sizes are available, use 3mm. 2.5mm sheet would be thinner than 12swg.

IMPERIAL STANDARD WIRE GAUGE AND MILLIMETRE EQUIVALENTS

SWG No.	Thickness in inches	Thickness in mm	SWG No.	Thickness in inches	Thickness in mm
0	.324	8.230	21	.032	.813
1	.300	7.620	22	.028	.711
2	.276	7.010	23	.024	.610
3	.252	6.401	24	.022	.550
4	.232	5.893	25	.020	.508
5	.212	5.385	26	.018	.457
6	.192	4.877	27	.0164	.416
7	.176	4.470	28	.0149	.378
8	.160	4.064	29	.0136	.345
9	.144	3.658	30	.0124	.315
10	.128	3.251	31	.0116	.295
11	.116	2.956	32	.0108	.274
12	.104	2.641	33	.0100	.254
13	.092	2.337	34	.0092	.234
14	.080	2.032	35	.0084	.213
15	.072	1.829	36	.0076	.193
16	.064	1.626	37	.0068	.173
17	.056	1.422	38	.0060	.152
18	.048	1.219	39	.0052	.132
19	.040	1.016	40	.0048	.122
20	.036	.914			

BENDING ALLOWANCE

INSIDE RADIUS, 90° BEND, INCH FRACTIONS	*Standard Wire Gauge* 25	24	23	22	21	20	19	18	17	16	15	14	13	12	11	10	9	8	7	6
Decimal inches	·020	·022	·024	·028	·032	·036	·040	·048	·056	·064	·072	·080	·092	·104	·116	·128	·144	·160	·176	·192
3/8	·605	·606	·608	·611	·614	·617	·620	·626	·632	·639	·645	·651	·661	·671	·679	·688	·702	·715	·728	·740
11/32	·556	·557	·559	·562	·565	·568	·571	·577	·583	·590	·596	·603	·612	·621	·631	·640	·653	·666	·678	·691
5/16	·507	·508	·510	·513	·516	·519	·522	·528	·534	·541	·547	·553	·563	·572	·582	·591	·604	·617	·630	·643
9/32	·458	·459	·461	·464	·467	·470	·473	·479	·485	·492	·498	·504	·513	·524	·533	·542	·555	·568	·581	·594
1/4	·408	·410	·412	·415	·418	·421	·425	·430	·436	·443	·449	·456	·465	·474	·484	·493	·506	·519	·532	·545
7/32	·359	·361	·363	·366	·369	·372	·375	·381	·389	·396	·402	·408	·418	·427	·437	·446	·459	·472	·485	·498
3/16	·310	·312	·314	·317	·320	·323	·326	·332	·338	·345	·351	·357	·367	·376	·386	·395	·408	·421	·434	
5/32	·262	·265	·268	·271	·275	·278	·284	·290	·297	·303	·309	·319	·328	·338	·347	·360	·373			
1/8	·212	·214	·216	·219	·222	·225	·228	·234	·240	·247	·253	·259	·269	·278	·288					
7/64	·188	·189	·191	·194	·197	·200	·203	·209	·215	·222	·228	·234	·244	·253						
3/32	·163	·165	·167	·170	·173	·176	·179	·185	·191	·198	·204	·210								
5/64	·139	·140	·142	·145	·148	·151	·154	·160	·166	·173	·179									
1/16	·114	·115	·117	·120	·123	·126	·130	·136	·142											
3/64	·089	·091	·093	·096	·099	·102	·105													
1/32	·065	·066	·071																	

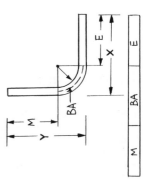

Length required for 90° bend
$M + BA + E$ where
$M = Y - (radius + thickness)$
$E = X - (radius + thickness)$
BA from table above

Figures are for malleable materials where neutral line lies at mid-thickness.

Bending allowance for angles over or under 90°
$$90° = \frac{90° \text{ figure from above} \times \text{Actual bend angle}}{90}$$

and for M and E (radius + thickness) becomes radius + thickness × tangent of half bend angle).

Judging the temperature of metals

It is often necessary to judge the temperature of metal while it is being heated. A good general guide to this under workshop conditions is the colour of the metal. Steel is especially good in this respect as it exhibits a wide range of oxide colours before it gets to red heat. Other metals only show a dull red to bright orange. The full range of colours is given at right, together with the approximate temperatures which they indicate.

Pale Yellow/light straw	230°C	Steel
Drk yellow/dark straw	240°C	
Brown	250°C	
Purple/Brown	260°C	Oxide
Dark purple	280°C	Colours
Blue	295°C	
Dark blue	300°C	
Faint red (in subdued light)	500°C	
Dull red	700°C	
Blood red	800°C	
Bright red	1000°C	
Orange	1200°C	
White	1400°C plus	

Bibliography

In the preparation of this book the following books have been found useful as sources of reference. Anybody who is interested in particular aspects of sheet metalwork may well find one or more of them of use. They are not listed in any special order.

'Basic Welding and Fabrication' – W. Kenyon. (Pitman)

'Engineering Workshop Practice' – Judge and Horner. (Caxton)

'Theory and Practice of Metalwork' – G. Love. (Longman's)

'Metalcraft in Theory and Practice' – J. R. Bedford. (Murray)

'Bodywork Maintenance and Repair' – P. Browne. (Autobooks)

'Geometric and Engineering Drawing' – K. Morling. (Arnold)

'Model Boilers and Boiler Making' – K. N. Harris. (Argus Books)

'Hardening and Tempering Engineer's Tools – Gentry and Westbury. (Argus Books)*

'An Introduction to Workshop Processes' – Gwyther and Page. (Penguin)

'Metals in the Service of Man' – Alexander and Street. (Pelican)

'Non-ferrous Metals Catalogue and Handbook' – (J. Smith & Sons [Clerkenwell] Ltd.)

'The Amateur's Lathe' – L. H. Sparey. (Argus Books)

'Metallurgy for Engineers' – E. C. Rollason. (Arnold)

(*Now superseded by 'Hardening, Tempering and Heat Treatment', Tubal Cain, from Argus Books).

Acknowledgements

I would like to thank the people named below who have helped with the production of this book in the ways described.

Mr Graham Jeeves and my father Mr R. Wakeford for help in checking manuscripts.
Miss C. Swietonioska for help with photography.
Mr M. Henks and Mr P. Williams for technical advice.
Mr M. Mabbs, Bsc, for technical advice and then checking the relevant parst of the manuscript.
Last, and by no means least, my mother, Mrs V. Wakeford, for checking and typing the manuscript.

Photo Credits

Photo 1	E. Jolliffe, Esq.
Photos 2, 4, 6, 7, 8, 9, 11, 12, 13, 14, 17	Miss C. Swietonioska
Photo 3	Hegner (U.K.) Ltd.
Photos 5, 10	Author
Photos 15, 16	Gabro Engineering Ltd.